I Saw Jesus in the Shower

By Julie Negri

Contents

Chapter 1: I'm Shrinking 6

Chapter 3: Summer Storms...21

Chapter 4: Singing in the Rain..29

Chapter 5: On My Knees..41

Chapter 6: Bombs are Dropped 46

Chapter 7: European Vacation 54

Chapter 8: Back to Reality. Wait, What? 64

Chapter 9: Confirmations..76

Chapter 10: The Thorn Appears..87

Chapter 11: Two by Fours..93

Chapter 12: Letting Go..103

Chapter 13: The Thorn Revealed 109

Chapter 14: Lessons 118

Epilogue..124

Endnotes...126

Chapter 1: I'm Shrinking

Everybody has a story to tell. If they're paying attention it can even be worth hearing. I'm sure there are many details that I'll miss, but seeing the Lord of the universe isn't one of them. Now let me just clear this up right off the bat. I was the one in the shower, not Jesus. He's the Lord of the universe. Why would He need a shower?

So, if you're wondering if He wears a shower cap, or uses a loofah, I've got nothing for you. But if you want to hear how your world can be rocked, I've got a story for you. I tried not telling it, for various reasons that you might understand a little if you keep reading. But God wouldn't let up.

First it was the Holy Spirit, and then it was Beth Moore at a Living Proof Live event. She was pretty adamant that we should tell our stories. I tried to ignore it, but the Holy Spirit wouldn't let up. I was convicted over and over again. Then I met a woman named Dorrie at my daughter's speech tournament. She encouraged me to write it all down. When I saw her a few months later at another tournament she told me that not only should I write it down, but that I should write the story the way I tell the story. I noticed that what little I had written already didn't really sound like me. So I rewrote it. I was told in so many ways that I had to write it down. If He got any clearer it would have been with a two by four. I have some experience with the two by four. It hurts. So I got writing.

So here I am. Two years from when the story began, and not 100% sure when it ended. Maybe it's still going on. So many wonderful blessings that flowed from my suffering, and still some hurts remain. But even those will be used to God's glory. Of that I can be sure. Experience has taught me that. Long before I saw Him in the shower, I knew I could trust Him. People? Not so much. But God? He's never failed me. He's never hurt me, or deserted me. He's only loved on me, and directed my path. On occasion I would listen. Other times I fought Him.

Sometimes you don't know for sure when a story starts. From the best I can tell, my story started at a point when my life was great. I was happily married and homeschooling my three kids. I had a great church family where I served as the Women's Ministry leader. Life was good.

A few months before, we had lived a dream that my husband, John, and I had long talked about. We started the school year driving around the country visiting National Parks and various landmarks and historical sites. We had talked about it since the kids were small. We decided at 13, almost 11 and 9, they were old enough to remember the experience. And we couldn't wait to get going. The trip was amazing. We traveled over 7000 miles, and the only problems we encountered were a little traffic outside Chicago and a bee sting. We knew and felt that the trip had been blessed. Even so, I had a sense of impending trouble. I didn't know what it would be, but I sensed from the Spirit that the trip was a gift. Something was coming. This knowing was scary. I was so fearful that I was going to lose someone. That I might be losing myself? That thought just never occurred to me.

My best guess is that the story began in February 2012. My grandmother, who had been living in a nursing home suffering from dementia, passed away. After my mother who was in Florida called in the early morning hours to tell me that the nursing home had called and she was failing fast, I quickly got dressed and got in the car. I hoped to make it there "in time." After about 10 minutes of driving, my cell phone rang. My sister who had made it there in time called to say it was over. My grandmother had passed away. I told her I would be there in a few minutes. After hanging up the phone I turned on the radio. Chris Tomlin's Amazing Grace was playing. The words to the song, "my chains are gone, I've been set free"[1] sank in.   She was free.

In the days that followed I learned that "Amazing Grace" was one of my grandmother's favorite songs....I'm pretty sure she never heard Chris Tomlin's version, but I knew God was using the song to speak to me. This is something He often does. The irony in that is that I am completely devoid of any musical talent, but I don't let that stop me. In the months that followed He would repeatedly use song lyrics to speak to my heart, and later to heal my broken spirit.

It was at her funeral that I first noticed that I had lost some weight. The pants I was wearing were loose, strangely so. They fit fine the last time I had worn them a few weeks prior. It was annoying, mainly because I wasn't at home and couldn't just change my outfit. When I got home from the funeral, I weighed myself out of curiosity. I had lost a little weight, about 5-6 pounds.

About a year and half before this time I had finally gotten around to losing the baby weight. My youngest was 7. It was time. But since then I had pretty much maintained a healthy weight. I didn't really have 10 pounds I needed to lose. I was good. Sure, I gained a bit around the holidays, but otherwise, my weight remained steady. That is until it didn't anymore.

I wasn't concerned, but decided it wouldn't hurt to go in for a check-up. So I called over and made an appointment to see my general practitioner, a woman I often recommended to others. She had always been responsive in the past, and I generally trusted her medical opinion. When I went in for the checkup she wasn't too concerned about the weight loss. She asked about stress, and although I didn't personally have any great stressors, there were some peripheral issues. My grandmother died, and we had a very sad incident in our extended family the month prior. But in our immediate family things were moving along pretty steady. I couldn't really identify any personal stressors that seemed that demanding. We just had the normal problems. Kids driving you crazy, all the running around....but nothing that I would think could cause physical symptoms. In fact we were kind of in a lull period between the busy sports schedule of the spring. The doctor decided to do some blood work, but she wasn't concerned since some blood work done in October was "picture perfect'"

She did comment that as a mom I probably wasn't eating well. I have to confess, there was some truth to this. Life gets much busier as the kids get older. It seemed we were always on the run from one activity to the next. Sometimes lunch was whatever I could grab: a banana, a yogurt...whatever was easy. So I resolved to be more intentional about what I was eating. I never eat breakfast except when I was pregnant or nursing. I hadn't since I was a kid. I decided to change this. As much as I don't like eating in the morning, I would be a good girl, and eat breakfast everyday. Nothing to worry about. I was just going to "eat more." Little did I know that within a few months the phrase "eat more" would bring me to tears.

After a week or so, I hadn't heard back from my doctor about the blood work, so I decided to give her a call. She has an online system where she can post lab results with her comments. She hadn't done this…but I was sure basic blood work had been completed. After two calls to the doctor to ask about the results, I got the receptionist who spoke with the doctor. She came back to report that everything "looked fine." While I would have preferred to have the doctor speak to me, it appeared that wasn't going to happen. The next day the lab results finally appeared on the website without comment. Everything "looked fine," so I was just going to go with that. I'd be more aware of what I was eating, keep up with the breakfasts, and surely the weight loss would stop.

It sounded like a simple plan….I'd just be more intentional, and all would be fine. Meanwhile, as the Women's Ministry leader at my church, I was praying about what study we should offer the ladies in the spring. We had a church-wide adult study that many women were involved in at the time.

As I prayed about it, I kept coming back to Brave: Honest Questions Women Ask, by Angela Thomas. The study had a DVD component, so I checked the listing of resources from our association's lending library. It wasn't listed. But God was being persistent so I decided to call and see if maybe they had it and it just wasn't on the list. When I called, I was told, "Julie, I literally just opened the package containing this study. It's sitting on my desk. I'll get it checked in, and in the mail to you tomorrow!"

Well, it seemed pretty clear to me that some woman in our church would need this study. She'd need to be brave. I should have asked more questions. It didn't even enter my mind that that woman might be me.

Meanwhile, I'm being a good girl. Making sure I ate the dreaded breakfast every day, lunch, and a good dinner. Snacking was never a problem. I love to snack. But strangely, the weight kept falling off. Now, I know people think this is a ridiculous thing to complain about, but it was concerning. Especially since I was so conscious of what I was eating. This was around the same time that people thought it was a good idea to tell me to gain weight, or eat more. It was very frustrating, and something I still don't quite understand. If someone gains 10 pounds, I don't think anyone would feel justified in telling them to lose some weight and eat less. But this was what I heard quite often. Even from people who were aware of the struggle. It was very strange, and something to which I didn't know how to respond, so I let it go and tried not to be offended. Life was busy, so I didn't really have much time to mull it over in my mind.

As I continued losing weight, it seemed clear to me that something was amiss. It wasn't normal. The busy mom theory was losing steam. I had been intentional about what I ate for a couple of months now. I couldn't pretend I was just so busy I probably wasn't eating well enough. The jig was up. Something was wrong. So in April I made another appointment with my doctor. I was down over 15 pounds by now, all while trying desperately to gain weight. She didn't seem the least bit concerned. My blood work from February was fine…so no worries…Just "Eat more." She also recommended I supplement my diet with Carnation Instant breakfasts to up the caloric intake and come back for a follow up in a month. Looking back now, it's shocking how dismissive she was about my symptoms. At this point I had lost over 15% of my body mass….all while trying to gain weight! If she was thinking I had an eating disorder, or somehow doing this to myself, perhaps screening me for such would have been more appropriate than looking the other way. If that what was she thought, shouldn't she have done something? I couldn't figure it out. My great love and respect for this particular doctor was diminishing rapidly.

Every person I spoke to who had any medical knowledge thought her response was absurd. After talking to my brother in law, a doctor, I decided to pursue things further on my own. Thankfully, my health insurance didn't require a referral for a visit to gastrointestinal doctor. I called several trying to get an appointment within a reasonable time frame. I reluctantly made an appointment for about a month later. The receptionist, upon hearing my symptoms, put me on a cancellation list. A few days later, I got the call for an opening later that week. I was a bit anxious, but relieved that I would hopefully get to the bottom of the problem.

The doctor was wonderful and took the symptoms seriously. That alone was a relief. He was very concerned by the weight loss, and felt a endoscopy and colonoscopy were in order. They had an opening a few days later, the day after Mother's Day. I figured, I might as well get it over with, although the "prep" made for a less than desirable Mother's Day.

The tests weren't nearly as traumatic as I feared...they knock you out pretty good. The doctor didn't see anything alarming, but there were a few biopsies we would have to wait to hear the results. I was just happy that I would be allowed to eat again! Overall I wasn't that concerned....there was no obvious problem, like say a tumor. So I figured the test results would show what was going on...Celiac or bacterial overgrowth were both possibilities. So more waiting. When the results came in a week later, they just deepened the mystery. They found absolutely nothing. No explanation for my symptoms.

Chapter 2: The Shower

Up until this point the weight loss was the only symptom. I felt fine; I just looked terrible as people were kind enough to tell me on a frequent basis. But now things were changing. Fatigue was setting in. In God's great mercy, the fatigue didn't start until the end of our homeschool year. It started out somewhat mild, but it would get much worse as the summer progressed.

When I went for the follow-up with my general practitioner, she seemed less than pleased that I had gone to see a specialist without being referred. I didn't care, because quite frankly, it was my health at stake, not hers. She noted that despite my supplementing my diet, I had still continued to lose weight. She palpitated my abdomen and decided a CAT scan was in order.

Apparently she felt a "mass" beneath my umbilicus. She said not to worry, it could just be my abdominal aorta and she could only feel it because of the weight loss. I asked if she felt a pulse. She had to reluctantly concede that she hadn't. Now, I'm not a doctor, but I knew enough to know that if it had no pulse, I was either dead, or it wasn't my aorta. I didn't appear to be dead, which left it wasn't my aorta. I had noticed the sense of "something being there" when I would lean in a certain direction, but just thought I could feel it because of the weight loss. Now I was worried. The word, "mass" didn't sound good to me.

So I foolishly got on Google. I don't recommend doing this. What I learned was that if the "mass" the doctor felt was in fact a tumor, it was bad news. Really bad. Tumors in this area are almost always metastasized from another location. The average survival time was 13 months. Now I was scared. I knew there was something there, I could feel it. I knew that despite my best intentions, I could not gain an ounce, let alone keep on the weight I had. And I was starting to feel sick, not just look sick. I was thankful that I was able to get an appointment for the CAT scan the following week.

Meanwhile we're working through the last week of the Brave study. The week's topic was "I am Broken." Seriously, God? But as ridiculous at things were seeming, the week's study was custom made for me. One of the points the author made was that we needed to choose to live for the glory of God. Looking through the book now, I see that I had highlighted and underlined a good portion of the week's study. I knew I wasn't being punished by God, but I didn't understand the whys of the struggle. I was following Him already, wasn't I? Why was this happening? It didn't seem fair, but I also knew Him and trusted Him. It was a strange week. But it was about to get stranger still.

The night before the CAT scan, a Tuesday night, I was in the shower. I was getting nervous, realizing that the following day I could be getting news that would be life changing, and not in a good way.

I'm someone who talks to God anywhere...anytime...He doesn't seem to mind. I thought the shower was as good place as any to let it all out. No kids around to traumatize with my tears. So I cried out to Him, and what happened next is almost impossible to describe, but I'll try.

As I lifted my hands in praise, I "saw" heaven open up for a brief moment. There was very bright light beaming down, and right there in the middle was Jesus, holding out His hand to me. His eyes....love poured out of His eyes, and His outstretched hand seemed to be beckoning me. It was just a second...so fast, yet so clear. I'll never forget it. To say it was startling is an understatement. Accompanying the vision was an indescribable sense of peace. The fear dissolved in an instant.

Now don't get me wrong. There was definitely a "what in the world just happened" moment. It wasn't your average rinse and repeat experience. It was earth shattering. I don't know about you, but I don't usually get an actual glimpse of heaven when I'm taking a shower. In fact, it's never even happened when I'm not in the shower. I've heard Him, felt Him, and experienced Him, but never before like that. My mind was boggled, but my soul was in a state of inexplicable peace.

Being a woman, I felt the need to analyze the experience to determine what it meant. It almost didn't matter what it meant, the experience was so real. So potentially life changing without need for understanding. But analyze I did. He was holding out His hand, and seemed to be calling me to Him. That seemed to mean one thing to me. There wasn't a sense of fear anywhere around the experience. Even so, I was sure the vision I had was God telling me that I would be home with Him soon. Still, the sense of peace was so pervasive and warming, I was able to sleep without worry.

The next day dawned, and John and I headed to the hospital for the CAT scan. I wasn't nervous anymore. The test was pretty quick. I tried to scope out the technician's facial expressions for a clue. Did she see a massive tumor? Was that a sympathetic look she just gave me? Apparently she had played this game before. She gave nothing away. So home we went and we had a totally normal day.

If I didn't know any better, I never would have believed a phone call could change my life at any moment. Homeschool, prepping for Bible Study, dinner, and then I was off to church. The irony of leading the session entitled, "I am broken" on that of all days was not lost on me. When the study ended that night a woman in the group approached me. She told me that she saw "the Spirit come down" on me as I was speaking. This sounded a bit weird to me, but then again I saw Jesus in the shower the night before. Who was I to think anything is weird?

So I headed home, pondering the strangeness of the past 24 hours. When I got home I checked my email and noticed a notification that test results had been posted on the online site that my doctor uses. It was the results of the cat scan! If I was analyzing things I would have guessed it was good news, or she would have called. I didn't pause long enough to analyze anything. I just clicked away to the results...which showed nothing. There was nothing there! The doctor's notes didn't provide much new information except that there was nothing found. I called my husband with the good news. After the shower experience, this was not the news I was expecting. Which begged the question: What was up with that? It sure looked like He was calling me home.

Of course I couldn't just let it go. That's not how I operate. I question and question. I want to know what's going on at all times. That night I was bold in my questioning. Thankful, but still wondering what the previous night's experience was all about. It wasn't your run of the mill shower.

Now, sometimes God speaks to His children through His word, through others, through circumstances, and at other times He just speaks. His sheep know His voice. That night, in response to my, "What was up with that, Jesus?" He simply told me: "I was showing you what you believe."

This was fabulous....It really was fabulous; I'm not being sarcastic here.   But, What???? I already thought I was pretty firm in what I believe. Of course getting a glimpse of eternity certainly didn't dim my faith. I'll have that experience to hold onto until I see Him again face to face. So it was certainly a life shaking moment. I appreciated that He gave it to me, but I didn't understand why. Why did I need to "see" the truth of what I believed? If it wasn't about the CAT scan, I was just confused. Perhaps it was the exclamation mark to the clean scan, and the fact that the weight loss seemed to have stopped. I was starting to feel "sick", but otherwise things seemed to be pointing to a positive. So for once I stopped with all my questions. And for once maybe I should have asked a few more.

Chapter 3: Summer Storms

Although the weight loss had stopped, other symptoms were just beginning to rear their ugly heads. I foolishly assumed that the weight loss had caught up with me and now that it had stopped I would, of course, start to feel better. The CAT scan was clear, and I thought I was in the clear as well. Yeah, not so much as it turns out.

My joy over the CAT scan results soon turned to confusion. The weight loss seemed to have stopped, the CAT scan was clear, so why am I now starting to feel so sick. Fatigue was kicking in, and dizziness followed me. What in the world? So I called the doctor again.

What was the next step? She was hesitant to do anything quite honestly. It was weird that she was the only person who didn't find my symptoms alarming. But she relented and ordered a chest x-ray, and some blood work. The following morning my family and I were heading up to an amusement park to meet up with some homeschool friends to celebrate the end of our school year. I got up early and headed up to the hospital to get the tests done. When I returned we got ready to head out for a fun day. Thankfully John had taken the day off from work, so he drove and was my leaning post. The kids had fun, but I was realizing how fatigued and dizzy I was getting. Little did I know this was just the beginning.

In His great mercy, the worst of it didn't kick in until we finished our homeschool year. When I hadn't heard from the doctor about the test results, I called. She eventually called me back. The x-ray was clear, nothing alarming to note. Apparently she was looking at the results for the first time while I was on the phone. She told me that I had a virus, CMV, which could explain things. Then she said, "Wait, you have mono!"

Mono? I don't know what happened to the CMV diagnosis from seconds ago, but Mono sounded good to me. With time Mono gets better. I could live with that diagnosis. It explains the sick feeling I was getting, if not the weight loss. She said as much. But her concern never was with the weight loss. It seems she thought I was willing my body to not absorb any nutrients…. As irritating as her attitude was, I was overjoyed to have an explanation. "Yay! I have mono!!!"

Or maybe not. In speaking with my doctor brother-in-law a few days later, I gave him the sign in for the website where my doctor would post my test results. Imagine my surprise and frustration when he called and said, "Good news! You don't have mono!"

I thought having mono was the good news! My brother in law explained that I was positive for having antibodies for both CMV and Epstein-Barr, the mono virus. But the test that detected a current infection was negative. So what that means is that at some point in my life, it could have been 20 years ago, I was exposed to both viruses. But I currently didn't have either. So much for the explanation. Now I was back to the great unknown.

After several phone calls my doctor called me back. But not until I left the message that my brother in law, who she knew, disagreed with her diagnosis. She was less than apologetic. She admitted that my brother in law's reading of my lab work was in fact correct. She explained that what "she meant" was that I may have had mono at some point. Her explanation didn't hold much weight, but since I couldn't order my own labs, I asked her to test me for Lyme Disease. It's pretty prevalent in my area, and I knew I had a tick bite a month back. She was surprised that I hadn't been tested for that yet. The fact that she was the one ordering the tests seemed to have been lost on her. So I got the test done, and the lab results were posted online without comment. Thankfully

I had a doctor in the family to interpret the results. They did not indicate a positive result.

At this point it was clear that I was in need of a new doctor. This was right around the time that the U.S. Supreme Court upheld the Affordable Care Act. It was not a good time to find a doctor taking new patients. But prayer can overcome anything. I was thankful after many calls to find a doctor taking new patients. She had worked in the Navy base in Newport, and was moving to the other side of the bridges. I was able schedule an appointment for late in July.

While the hunt for a new doctor was ongoing, we were working to organize a fiftieth anniversary party for my parents. Their anniversary would be in August, when they would be taking all of us….my six siblings, their spouses, and grandchildren to Ireland for a once in a lifetime family vacation. With so many siblings, we were able to split the work of creating a great celebration. One of the major things I was working on was creating a DVD slideshow set to music. This was a big project, but thankfully my husband did a great deal of the work. We spent many hours working together in his office. Although I was exhausted at times, I didn't seem to be getting any worse. The party went off without a hitch. It was great to see so many cousins, aunts and uncles. Little did I know that within a month I would be thinking it had been for one last time. I spent the month of June tired and some days bedridden, but I was still expecting to be feeling better soon.

Living in Rhode Island we always spent time at the beach. In June, I decided to purchase a lakeside membership to a nearby YMCA. This was a nearby option for summer fun that I knew would be easier on me than day trips to the ocean. This single decision helped make the summer bearable for my children. My plan was that I would of course start feeling better, and we'd have some real beach days in the mix. This was just a little insurance policy. I also knew that quite a few fellow homeschoolers belonged. Looking back I see this simple decision was a gift. As the summer progressed my fatigued increased. We never did end up making it to the ocean at all that summer.

As July started, I was hopeful that things would get better eventually. At least they didn't seem to be getting any worse. As it turns out July could best be described my Dickens' famous line: It was the best of times, it was the worst of times.

Early in July, I was lying in bed praying. This seemed to be a common activity that year. The Lord spoke to my heart as clearly as if He was standing next to me. I heard His voice, and it didn't sound like the best news. It also didn't sound like the worst news. He has a way of keeping me calm. "You're going to go through this, and it's going to get hard. But I will show myself to people through it"

I foolishly thought it was already pretty hard. But wait, it was going to get worse! Yay! That He would use this and show Himself was a nice thought, though. I had list of people He could use this trial to reveal Himself, so this was exciting news. As it turns out, He had His own list. Looking back now, I'm amazed that most of the people He showed Himself to through my struggle were people I didn't even yet know. In the end I was more surprised by the people who already knew Him that refused to acknowledge His hand in the outcome. But I'm jumping ahead here.

By this time, I couldn't predict how I would feel one day to the next. Most days I was very tired, but others it rose to the level of "fatigued." On those days it was debilitating. Other days however I could be somewhat functional. These are the days we took advantage of and went to the YMCA, or out to get some errands done. It was a very frustrating time as I felt I couldn't make any plans. One day I was functional, the next bedridden. There seemed to be no rhyme or reason to it.

It began as a gradual decline. First I was losing weight, then I was losing more and dizzy....then I was feeling just sick, and fatigued....little by little. Perhaps that's why it was so hard for people to see what was going on. One friend from church told me that she didn't realize how sickly I had become until her daughter returned home from college and wanted to know what was wrong with me. It was then that she looked at me and was shocked to realize how sickly I had become.

There were 2 upcoming events that weighed heavy on my mind. We had the big family trip to Ireland coming up in about a month and a half, and the wedding of a dear "not technically a niece, but like a niece" friend, Tina. I asked God many times to keep me able to attend both.

In his mercy, I had one of my "just tired" days on her wedding day. It was very encouraging. Maybe I was on my way back to feeling normal. I finally had the appointment with the new general practitioner coming up. Maybe we were getting somewhere.

When the appointment arrived I was relieved to feel comfortable. She spent a good deal of time reviewing my symptoms and lab reports. She clearly found things to be disturbing, and ended up ordering a host of other labs. Some I had drawn at a lab in her building, others I had to return to have drawn in the morning. I was hopeful that we would finally get somewhere. I had had a "good" weekend....I was hopeful that I would somehow be able to enjoy the upcoming Ireland trip. Things were about to go downhill fast.

The weeks that followed found me struggling daily to do basic things. Dinners often became burgers on the grill cooked up by my husband. A good deal of my time was spent in bed. Often my youngest daughter, who was 9 at the time, would join me. We watched quite a bit of Little House on the Prairie those days, and for some reason Jurassic Park. On days when I was up to it, we would head over to the YMCA lake. It didn't require much, but still it was a challenge. We would park the car and walk a short distance across the grassy field that stood between the lot and the beachfront area. I found I had to pause several times on the short walk to regain my balance. Things were getting more and more disturbing.

That's when I started to notice the bruising. Lots of it....big bruises on my legs, my arms, my back even. Apparently all that lying in bed and sleeping was hazardous. I was in bad shape and I knew it. This wasn't some weird virus as I was trying to tell myself. I had become a skeleton. A waif who couldn't walk across a room without being intentional, and often pausing to regain my balance. My brain was shutting down too. I remember one instance in particular. My pastor asked me to come to a meeting with a representative of a local ministry outreach. I thought, "I can do this. It's just a meeting."

Turns out I should have declined. I'm pretty sure the woman thought I was on drugs. I don't know if I was coherent, but I know I couldn't hold a thought, and the drive home was a challenge. I was becoming a dizzy chick in more ways than one...and now I'm covered in bruises.

Something was really wrong. I just keep asking God to make me feel better, to protect the kids, and help John with all of it. It was a lot on his shoulders. Not just all he had to do at home, but also reality was sinking in for both of us. I was in big trouble. And he loves me. It may have been harder on him. After all, I saw Jesus in the shower. I had that to hold onto, while he was watching me slip away.

Chapter 4: Singing in the Rain

Throughout this time God continued to stalk me with songs. One morning I had to bring my youngest for an emergency dental appointment. She had a tooth that was broken. As we drove Casting Crowns song, "Praise You in This Storm" came on the radio. I could so relate. I didn't know where the storm was headed, or when it would end, but I knew I could still praise Him.

"I'll praise You in this storm

And I will lift my hands

For You are who You are

No matter where I am

Every tear I've cried

You hold in Your hand

You never left my side

And though my heart is torn

I will praise You in this storm"[2]

We stopped at the post office on the way for a quick errand. When we got back in the car, and started driving, the song came on again! Same station, same song 15 minutes later. Some might think it was a mistake on the station's part, but I knew it was the hand of God encouraging me to keep praising Him.

Throughout the trial, time and time again God used song to encourage and hold me up. Praising Him was the only solution to my pain...my fear...I used to kitchen dance, as I called it, daily. By this point I was more of a kitchen swayer, than dancer...but I could still praise Him Time and time again He used Mercyme's "Hurt and the Healer," to give me hope. I was hurt in many ways, but I knew the healer. I knew Him. I trusted Him, but like the song, I questioned the whys of it. God had told me that He would show Himself, but what about me? Would there be anything in it for me? What about my kids, and my husband? There didn't seem to be any answer forthcoming. So I just kept kitchen dancing, sometimes from a chair... but praising Him seemed to be the only reasonable response. Whenever I starting feeling like it was getting hopeless, He played the song for me, and restored my hope.

One song He used more than once was Casting Crown's "Voice of Truth." When the voices of those who would say hurtful things started, He would give me this song to steady me. And boom!...I was at the foot of the cross.

"Oh what I would do to have

The kind of faith it takes to climb out of this boat I'm in

Onto the crashing waves

To step out of my comfort zone

To the realm of the unknown where Jesus is

And He's holding out his hand

But the waves are calling out my name and they laugh at me

Reminding me of all the times I've tried before and failed

The waves they keep on telling me

Time and time again. 'Boy, you'll never win!'

You'll never win"

But the voice of truth tells me a different story

And the voice of truth says "Do not be afraid!"

And the voice of truth says "This is for My glory"

Out of all the voices calling out to me

I will choose to listen and believe the voice of truth"[3]

I had voices on every side. On one side were the voices telling me it was my fault somehow. They would say they were praying, but I couldn't help but wonder what they asked God for on my behalf. Then there were the voices that came from genuine concern. They were actually very useful. But they weren't the truth either. There was my own voice, sometimes condemning myself, but mostly just calling out to God. And then there was the voice of God. The last time I saw him he had His hand out.

If I had to pick one voice to listen to, I was going to go with God. I knew I couldn't be trusted, and the people who thought I should "just eat more" really didn't comprehend the problem. I was realizing that God was the only one in any position to tackle the problem at this point. He said "Do not be afraid," so I wouldn't be. He told me that He had the whole situation in His hand. It was all for His glory. I had to go with that. His voice was saying to keep going and He'd meet me there. He just didn't tell me where "there" was. It was all for His glory. I just had to keep trusting, and press on a little longer.

I still can't believe how He was able to calm the Rolodex that would have otherwise been my mind. If you are a woman, or have ever met a woman, you know what I'm talking about. I could have been mentally reviewing every slight I ever received. Instead the Rolodex closed and stayed that way for months.

Looking back I can now see many ways that He used this in my family life. My inability to complete normal tasks resulted in us changing how things were done. Most of the time during this period, my husband would take on grocery shopping, but some days I would do it. Rather than go alone, as I used to do, I would bring the girls with me. I would lean on the shopping cart to keep myself upright, while they gathered the groceries we needed. Rachel, my oldest, is a great shopper as it turns out. She'll compare prices on different brands, and check volumes. Often times my youngest would bring over something, and before I said a word, Rachel would pipe in about the price of the item...I didn't have to say a word, although I would sometimes overrule Rachel's frugal ways when chocolate was involved. This has carried over to today. Most times when I mention the need to shop, Rachel will voluntarily come with me.

Any mom of a teen knows that this time is a gift, and I don't disregard the fact that God created new habits in my family through this time of struggle.

There were also things that were not so obvious in their "blessings" value. It was a time of realizing just how alone I was in this. Interestingly, it was after the trial seemed to be over that this aloneness, and the associated hurts became a real issue. That's when the spiritual battle began. While I was sick, I had my eyes so focused on Christ that nothing else mattered.

In the midst of it, our world became very small. Apart from the YMCA and an occasional errand, I rarely left the house except to attend church. When your world gets that small you find out how much you like each other. Can you really keep your sanity if it's just you and your family? With John working at home, we spend more time together than most other couples already. It just became a little bit more. Like all of the time. I think we managed just fine. Despite the physical hardship and the worry, we were happy. Very happy. Strangely so, considering the circumstances. As it turns out, we really like each as much as we love each other.

I don't want to give you the wrong impression. This wasn't some made for TV, "disease of the week" love story. The dying woman's wayward husband repents and comes back to her and loves her back to good health. That wasn't the case here, although he certainly had an amazing ability to keep it all in perspective. I think it was around this time I coined the phrase "the Juliewhisperer." While others frustrated me by pretending there was nothing wrong, he knew all too well that we had a problem. A big one. He didn't pretend it wasn't happening, and he definitely didn't blame me and try to make me feel badly. At the same time he wasn't running around like a chicken with his head cut off declaring the sky was falling. I'm sure he had some moments when I wasn't looking, but he seemed to keep everything in perfect balance. I don't know if I would have fared as well if it hadn't been for that.

We were already happy, and for most part aware of how blessed we were when it began. In the same way that He takes bad things and uses them for good, God can take things that are already good, and make them better. He's amazing like that.

That's what He did here. Given our lifestyle, John working at home and me home with the kids full time, we had the baseline of obviously liking each other already. If not we probably wouldn't still be married. Or one of us would be buried in a shallow grave. Thankfully we really like each other apart from all the love stuff. As I tell my kids: It's more important to like the person you're married to, than it is to love them. In our situation it was even more important due to the unusual amount of time we spend together.

Even so, it was hard to go through something like this feeling so alone and isolated from the rest of the world. No one seemed to care other than to make sure I knew that I looked horrible. At the same time, it was amazing to see clearly how loved I am by my husband. My best friend, and as it turned out one of a very few people who truly cared about me. It seemed my value to most everyone else was calculated in what I could do for them. When I was taken out of commission, people disappeared. But not John. The sicker I got, the more he made sure I knew how much he loved and valued me. I could do little for him, and still he adored me. I am truly blessed, and God used this time to shine a light on that fact.

It was also during this time that I found the deepest intimacy with Jesus. He met me every day. In his word, of course...but in a deeper way....everyday He spoke to my heart, and kept me full of hope and yes, even joy. To have the Lord of the universe reach down to comfort and encourage you every day was a gift. Something to be treasured. It made it all worth it, even if that was all I was to gain through the trial. Spiritual blessings are almost impossible to describe. To feel His supernatural peace in the midst of fear and despair is something that defies logic and words. It just is. He topped it off with His very real and obvious presence as He walked with me day by day through the darkness.

One evening I was thinking about my day as only a woman could. I was all set to give God an earful about an unkind comment that had been said to me that day at church, but I didn't get very far. I only needed to ask, "Did you hear what she said to me?"

I was immediately enveloped in His love and gently told, "Yes, I did, and it's mine to deal with."

My normal female response would be to demand to know how He was going to deal with it, and to be sure He fully understood what I was telling Him. I could have easily gone on and on about this, but instead He stopped me in my tracks, and I was completely at peace about it.

"Great, God. You deal with her." And I just let it go. This is not a normal response for me. I want details. "Did you smack her upside the head? What are you doing about it?" I wanted to go on and on about how hurt I was, and how wrong she was, but God had a better plan. I let it go, and went to sleep.

By the grace of God alone, His gentle reply soothed by hurting heart. Keeping my eyes on Him was much more productive. Anyway, I was the one who probably deserved the smack upside the head. Who was I to demand anything of God? Let alone demand He deal with someone's sin? Amazing that He could so easily soothe my outrage, and turn my heart back where it belonged. I would have smacked me upside the head if I were Him.

That was the beauty of this time period. I actively felt the presence of God EVERY DAY. It was palpable, and uplifting. In fact the sicker I felt physically, the more confident and joyful I felt spiritually. You wouldn't think that would make any sense, but somehow it did. His peace just followed me. Perhaps it was because I was getting closer and closer to seeing face to face what I saw in the shower that night. What I saw from a distance was drawing near.

Even as things progressed and I knew I was in trouble, the prayers of my Christian brothers and sisters upheld me. I remember one night in particular. I wasn't in "trust God" mode at that moment. I was in "poor me" mode. I was feeling pretty low physically, and lamenting that I must be weak. I mean, maybe the people were right who thought that if I just took better care of myself, I'd be fine. That must be it. I'm weak.

No sooner did the thought pass my consciousness, when I "saw" my house surrounded by prayer warriors. Arrows were plinking off their shields, and I was able to let the thought go. Although I couldn't see any faces, I knew who those warriors were.

One Sunday in particular, I was a bucket of tears. To a certain extent it was in a good way, despite my frustrations. The music that week had me overcome with His presence. The message was about persevering in the race of faith. Keep following Jesus, and persevere. I went forward at the invitation and my Pastor prayed for me. I was just worn out and losing any hope that I would get better. On the way out of church that day, John noted that if there was any chance we weren't believing God, that was now gone after the service. We would have to have been completely unaware to not see the hand of God at work.   We both knew God was speaking to us, and encouraging us specifically. We had to keep believing and waiting for His glory to shine through. But it wasn't going to be easy.

There are times I may have traumatized folks with my leaky eye syndrome. It seemed for the most part to occur whenever someone asked me how I was doing. Usually this was at church, since I rarely went anywhere else. Often times it was men, which probably made it all the more traumatic for them. Some poor unwitting man would earnestly ask how I was doing, and my eyes would start leaking! Women for the most part had the good sense to simply hug me and tell me they were praying. I guess they had no need to ask how I was doing. One look at me said it all.

I especially traumatized my nephew one day. Poor guy innocently said "Hey Auntie, How are you doing?" When he lifted his head and looked at me, he met my tears. Such things are especially traumatic to 23 year old nephews. My poor sister in law got an earful about that.

Apart from the leaky eyes, I was holding up pretty well emotionally. I made an art form out of making the best of things. When I was up to it, we'd head over to the lake. Whenever we had the opportunity to grab a little fun, we did.

The trip was coming up quickly, and I was going downhill at a record pace. At this point the wisdom of traveling had to be addressed. John was rightly concerned. Was it a good idea to leave the country in my condition? It actually seemed like a ridiculous thing to do at this point, even though I was traveling with a doctor, my brother-in-law. We were getting very discouraged. Any upswing I had experienced was long gone. I was heading downhill fast. What if something happened while we were out in the countryside? Going away was looking like a completely irresponsible thing to do. On the other hand, my family had been talking about this trip for at least 5 years. My parents, all of my siblings, their spouses, the grandkids....23 people in all. And we were seriously thinking of bailing. My kids would be devastated, as would my parents. It was a celebration of their 50th anniversary, and everyone should be there. We didn't know what to do.

About a week or so after my appointment with the new doctor, I received a letter informing me that the lab work had shown some endocrine issues, and a visit to an endocrinologist was in order. I called the list of doctors they sent. I ended up making an appointment with several doctors....anything I could find. The appointments I could get were months out. Finally, I called one office that could give me an appointment in about a month. Unfortunately, it was during the time period when we would be in Ireland. They were able to accommodate me, and give me an appointment 5 days before we were scheduled to leave. It was a relief to have an appointment, and we decided that we would wait for my upcoming appointments to make a decision about canceling the trip.

Chapter 5: On My Knees

One night in early August, John was down stairs watching a movie with the kids. I was playing a Youtube video, listening to the Tenth Avenue North song, "Hold My Heart." I was really feeling it. The song was aptly describing where I was, or I thought so anyway.

"How long must I pray

Must I pray to You?

How long must I wait

Must I wait for You?

How long till I see Your face

See You shining through, I'm on my knees

Begging You to notice me

I'm on my knees, Father, will you turn to me"[4]

And then the phone rang. I paused the song, and looked at the phone. The caller ID revealed it was a call from my doctor's office. I answered and found that it was my new doctor's partner. My doctor was on vacation. The partner was calling to check up on me. Her questions were downright disturbing. Why was she calling me and asking all these questions ...about breathing...about vertigo ...the fatigue, the lack of sleep, my vision....and on and on. I didn't know it at the time, but there was a reason for the concerned call. A new batch of lab results had come in, and it was all bad news....very bad news. She didn't tell me this at the time, but I knew she was obviously very concerned. When the call ended, John came upstairs to see what the call was all about. I just fell into his arms, "I'm in trouble." I just knew it.

After telling him about the conversation he tried to find something hopeful about the call. Maybe we just weren't used getting good healthcare and that's why the concerned call seemed so strange. I let him go with that thought, although I knew otherwise. He went downstairs to rejoin the kids, and I put the music back on. After the scary, concerned phone call, the song was all the more relevant:

"   One tear in the driving rain

One voice in a sea of pain

Could the maker of the stars

Hear the sound of my breaking heart

One life, that's all I am

Right now I can barely stand If

You're everything You say You are

Would You come close and hold my heart

I've been so afraid, afraid to close my eyes

So much can slip away before I say goodbye

But if there's no other way I'm done asking why

I'm on my knees begging You to turn to me

I'm on my knees Father, will you run to me"[4]

Now I'm really feeling like God is right there next to me. And then it hit me. I wasn't on my knees. And of all the things I asked God for that summer, I hadn't actually asked Him to heal me. Kind of crazy when I considered how much time I spent with Him that summer. I asked Him to make me feel better, to be able to attend certain events, and to make things easier on my family. I'm not sure why that is, other than I must have been in denial about how bad things were getting.

But as the past few weeks testified, there was no denying it at this point. I was sick, probably very sick.

So I made my way upstairs, and dropped to the floor by my bed. For some reason the "on my knees" part seemed very important. It wasn't my usual prayer posture, but something about being small before God in that moment seemed so right.

I was at His mercy, in more ways than one. I didn't beat around the bush, or offer up a multiple choice prayer for Him to choose a reply. Instead I begged Him to "take it out of me." I don't know why I choose those words, but it's what I cried out.

I think it was the Holy Spirit interceding. There was no multiple choice game of "heal me," or if not, "give me strength." I wasn't looking for strength. I wanted to be whole and healed again. So I begged for just that. That he would "take it out" and heal me.

Now I won't know this for sure until heaven, but I think that He healed me right then and there. It would be a week before a doctor would tell me that there was something that needed to be "taken out," but I think He healed me in that moment.

All the circumstantial evidence points to that. We see it in the Bible. When people threw themselves at the mercy of Jesus and asked for healing, He never made them wait. He just spoke it into being, and it happened. I think that's what He did for me. Looking back, knowing all I would come to learn and experience, it's the only thing that makes sense.

Over the next week, I began to feel a little more functional. I attributed it not to a healing, but to my wanting to be better so badly. Sheer will power. Did you see what I just did there? I boldly ask, even beg, God to heal me. And when I start feeling better I attribute it to ME!! Go ahead, judge me...I would.

That Sunday at church I knew my youngest, Olivia, was struggling. As much as I liked to think otherwise, the kids saw me wasting away and they were scared. At the end of service there is a time where people can go forward for prayer with the Pastor, or just kneel and pray themselves. Olivia and I went forward, and we prayed together. Actually, I prayed. After I finished, I asked Olivia if she was going to pray. She told me that she didn't need to pray anymore. I thought that was strange, but we went back to our seats.

When the service was over, I asked why she didn't need to pray anymore. She said, "Because when you were praying, God told me that He would heal you."

My only response to this was, "Did He say when?" I was happy that she seemed more relaxed, and less worried, but I was losing patience.

Chapter 6: Bombs are Dropped

The trip was looming. Decisions had to be made.
Exactly one week before we were scheduled to leave, I
had a follow up with my general practitioner. Her nurse
asked if I had been able to make an appointment to see
the endocrinologist. When I told her I had an
appointment in two days she was shocked. "You got an
appointment that quickly? Who do you know?" So I
told her who I knew. She seemed either confused, or
impressed by my response. I'm not sure which.

I had managed to lose a few more pounds since my last visit. By now I was down 20 pounds. I was skeletal. On the upside, the downward spiral of the last few weeks seemed to be at a standstill. I was even starting to feel a little better. Not as dizzy, and while still tired, I no longer had the mind numbing fatigue that I had been battling. I knew that could change at any minute. The doctor was pleased that I had booked an appointment to see the endocrinologist. She said she thought the trip should be OK, especially since I was traveling with a doctor. She did ask that I talk it over with the endocrinologist at my upcoming appointment.

She asked the same disturbing questions as her partner had when she called me the week earlier. When I mentioned that, she told me that some new lab results had come in and they were more concerning. Rather than grill her about the possible implications of the test results, I let it go. So not me, but I was choosing to focus on the "It's OK to go on vacation," part of the visit. She made some copies of lab results for me to have. I made a follow-up appointment, and headed home.

So now I was in "figure out what we need for vacation" mode. It was a nice distraction. I somehow managed to not obsess about the upcoming appointment. I wouldn't say I was feeling good, but I was definitely feeling like maybe I was turning a corner. Hey, I was walking across rooms without needing to pause to steady myself. Progress.

When the day of the appointment with the endocrinologist arrived, John asked if I wanted him to come with me. I didn't think that was necessary. He had work to do, and would be taking 2 weeks vacation starting the next day. He had a lot of loose ends to tie up before he left. He was heading up to Foxboro with our son to see a Patriots game that night, so he was better off staying home and getting things done. For some reason I wasn't expecting anything earth shattering to happen at the appointment. I had been feeling better over the course of the last week...what could the doctor possibly say that I would need John with me?

As I drove to his office, I was running through the list of all I needed to accomplish in the next 4 days. So much to get done! I wasn't that worried about the appointment. I was just hoping for the "travel OK." As I pulled into the parking lot a song that I loved but hadn't heard in a while, Jeremy Camp's "I Still Believe," came on the radio. So I sat in the car and listened.

"Scattered words and empty thoughts seem to pour from my heart

I've never felt so torn before seems I don't know where to start

But it's now that I feel your grace fall like rain

From every fingertip, washing away my pain

I still believe in your faithfulness   I still believe in your truth

I still believe in your holy word even when I don't see, I still believe

Though the questions still fog up my mind with promises I still seem to bear

Even when answers slowly unwind It's my heart I see you prepare"[5]

It was when he got to the line: "Even when answers slowly unwind, It's my heart I see you prepare," that I knew hearing this song at this moment in time was no coincidence. I sang along as tears ran down my face. Strangely they weren't really tears of despair. They were tears of awe, as I sat in the presence of God in the parking lot of the doctor's office.

As the song continued, the words penetrated my heart. I knew he had written the song as a young newlywed who had just lost his wife to cancer. Despite the knowing of the moment, I also knew that I wasn't alone in this. He was right there by my side, and He'd carry me if He had to.

"The only place I can go is into your arms

Where I throw to you my feeble prayers

In brokenness I can see that this was your will for me

Help me to know you are near"[5]

My heart was being prepared for whatever I was about to be told. And in that moment, I knew it. When the song ended, I did the only things left to do. I thanked God for His faithfulness, pulled myself together, and walked into the building. He came with me.

I didn't have to wait long, but distracted myself with a magazine. I was called in, weighed and waited for the doctor. There were some issues with the forwarding of test results to his office, so he reviewed my symptoms and examined me while he waited to the final faxes to arrive.

As he looked over the lab reports he looked up at me and asked if I had any children. When I replied that I had three children that I homeschooled, he looked like I had slapped him. He actually seemed to recoil a bit. He then pulled it together and told me that my labs were very specific. The only way I could have Cortisol levels this high was if I had tumors secreting it into my bloodstream. There were really only 2 options. I either had a benign tumor, most likely in my pituitary gland, called Cushings Disease, or I had small cell carcinoma somewhere in my body. He then went on to tell me that based in my symptoms he would highly doubt Cushings which is characterized by weight gain. There was a very slight chance that a benign tumor elsewhere could cause these lab results, but again the symptoms didn't match. The most reasonable explanation was malignancy. We just had to find it. He was very straightforward with me. Going easy on me or holding back didn't seem to be his style.

I think it's important to note at this point that I wasn't freaking out, not even a little. I was trying to get all the information out of him that I could, but somehow kept a clear head. The same girl that may have looked a little desperate crying in the car, is now sitting in the doctor's office being told she is likely riddled with cancer, and I'm in complete control. Having seen Jesus in the shower came in handy at times like that.

I managed to ask intelligent questions. It was like we were talking about someone else. If we were talking about me, I should be crying, or something. Instead I was feeling safe in God's hand, and managed to ask the questions. The answers kind of sucked, but still I was safe in His hand.

The doctor was actually in favor of us taking the trip when he heard the circumstances. In the meantime he would await the result of a set of labs he was ordering that could hone in on where the tumors might be, and start to work with the insurance. I asked what would happen when I returned from the trip. He said, "When you get back we'll find the tumors."

Because I tend to notice things, I did notice that he said, "Find the tumors," not "Look for a tumor." He had been very forthright, and I know it was intentional. The "tumor markers" weren't just there, they were through the roof. He clearly thought I had cancer. And lots of it.

So the next step was to head down to the lab. I would return the next day for more lab work. When we got home from the trip, he'd have the results, and we could start the tumor hunt. But first we'd go to Europe....no question at this point....We were going. All my concerns about the wisdom of going were wiped away. One last vacation, and this one would not just be with my kids and husband.. I'd have my parents, siblings and nieces and nephews to enjoy. No question. We were going.

I called John and gave him a brief overview promising more details when I got home. I saved the bomb dropping for then. Just to make sure I knew He was there, God showed up again when I got in the car to go home. I turned on the radio, and the first thing I heard was "Hold My Heart" by Tenth Avenue North, the song that had brought me to my knees a week earlier. You would think I'd immediately become the girl crying in the car again. But I didn't. Instead I just sat back and listened. That would be the work of the Holy Spirit.

I really wasn't afraid. My gut reaction was a bit surprising. I actually felt a degree of relief. The decision was made in an instant as to whether we were going to Ireland. And now I knew we would find out what was wrong. It didn't sound like it was going to be good news, but at least we could start dealing with it. Plus, I saw Jesus in the shower.. so there was that. I knew whatever the outcome, He had it in His outstretched hand, and I would be OK. Maybe OK in heaven, but still OK.

When I got home it only took a quick Google search to recognize the symptom list of metastasized cancer as I researched small cell carcinoma. "Unexplained weight loss, fatigue, loss of appetite...." Hmmmm..... This is all sounding a bit too familiar. It quickly spreads and is highly fatal. Only 6% survived 5 years. 22% made it a year....The stats didn't leave me with much hope. It certainly explained the doctor's serious and ominous attitude. I also think this may have factored into the doctor's recommendation that we go ahead with the trip. It was looking like this could be my last vacation.

Chapter 7: European Vacation

John and I are "vacation people." We've made that a priority for years. We save up money we could spend on other things, and take great vacations. I'm sure our kids' memories of their childhood will be highlighted by the trips we've taken over the years. A few months before this trial started, we had the Big Trip....A road trip around the US. Now we'd go to Ireland and London. It was a great distraction, I think. I had to get organized for the trip, no time to deal with reality. I did need prayer, though.

In asking for prayer I had to be selective. I didn't want my kids to see it on the prayer list, or hear someone talking about it. I sent out prayer requests to specific people. I have to confess, I did emphasis the "could be benign" much more than the doctor did. He had been very frank about the weight issue, and what that meant. I don't know if that was denial, or me trying to put off what seemed to be the inevitable. But I knew that God knew the tumor situation, I just wanted to not have them in my body. I didn't care if they were cancer or not.

I think I picked the right people to go to for prayer. I know at least two people, both named Lisa interestingly, who let God have an earful. One of the Lisas even yelled at Him. I have other friends who I knew went boldly to the throne on our behalf. It's actually a very comforting experience to know and feel people praying for you. I'm pretty sure this is what held me upright over the next few days.

There were other people who I did not want to know about my situation. Most especially my parents and kids. The trip was years in the planning and dreaming. I wasn't going to ruin it. So John was really the only one who truly knew the extent of what was going on. Everyone else got the version that would have them praying, but maybe not worrying so much.

These are the times that you have conversations with your spouse that you wish you weren't having. I'd tell you about it, but I won't. That's too private But suffice it to say, I'm a very blessed person. It was going to suck for John when I was gone, because I'm pretty awesome, too.

In my years as a Christian wife, I've always known that God wants a wife to put her husband first, right after Christ. A Christian husband is supposed to do the same and then some. I have to admit, it just didn't seemed practical as parents. What about the little people who need to be held and fed and cared for everyday? In the middle of this storm the center of my family became so clear to me. Finally I got it, and understood. Turns out God knows what He's talking about.

While the kids' lives were about to have them starring in a sad Disney movie, they'd still have a parent. They'd be sad, and struggle when I was gone, but their father would take care of them. They wouldn't be left alone. John on the other hand, wouldn't still have a wife, or a best friend, or a partner. He'd be alone with all of my responsibilities on top of his own. The kids had him. I saw Jesus in the shower, so I knew what was next for me. But what about him?

It may have looked like bad timing, but I think in reality it was God's perfect timing. I had so much to do for the trip which seemed all the more important now. That left little time to obsess. Research? Yes. Obsess? No. Although quite a bit of what I had to do was menial.

That left a lot of time for thinking. Despite all the thinking, I was handling all of it remarkably well. I had this vacation as a buffer between today and reality. I like buffers.

So for the next few days I made lists, ran errands, and folded mountains of laundry. I did have a lot to consider, but I managed to think things through in a fairly rational manner. School was going to be a big problem. Rachel, my oldest, had been to Kindergarten before we started to homeschool in first grade, but the other two had never been to school. Suddenly being thrust into the public school realm was going to be a big adjustment. I had already ordered our curriculum for the coming school year, so I didn't see the need to make any big changes to the plan just yet. Doing so would mean telling the kids what was going on. I wasn't ready for that. We would start the year at home, and where things went from there was a decision for another time. I knew if things looked like they were going to proceed quickly, we'd have to put them in school sooner. If they were going to lose their mother, I wanted to have things settled for them as much as possible before I left. So much to think about, but I knew the trip had to be the immediate concern. Everything else could wait.

Sunday showed up, and I was expecting a lot of weepiness at church. As it turned out I did pretty well. I cried more in the weekly services that summer, than I did that day. I was pretty good since I had turned my focus to the trip. 5 people to get ready for a 10 day, 2 country vacation. It definitely kept my mind busy. That

Sunday was the day before Vacation Bible School started. The girls would go for one day that week before we left on Tuesday. Rachel would serve, and Olivia would attend. The decorating set up was happening after Service. This actually worked out nicely. I didn't do much that could be called helpful, but having people lingering after service was nice. The people who knew what was going on were such an encouragement. It was good to head out with hugs, knowing that they had my back in prayer.

At one point I was talking to some friends, a mother and daughter, who knew about the tumor report. At least they knew as much as I was telling anyone apart from John. As I was talking to them I realized it was probably in my brain. My abdomen, my lungs, my intestines and stomach had all been either x-rayed or scanned. The doctor had told me that didn't rule out those areas. It starts small, but spreads quickly. Still, I felt pretty safe about those cancers. I was a few months into the trial when all that testing was done. I'd have thought they would have been able to see something at that point. The fact that I seemed to be losing IQ points was not something I could discount as easily. Add in the vertigo, the exhaustion, and the lightheadedness and I was putting my money on a brain tumor.

As I was about to leave someone who was in the know about the tumor report gave me a hug, and told me ....drum roll please....to gain some weight! I was good until that point. Really? The doctor tells me I have tumors, and the response is to continue to berate me about the weight loss? I managed to not cry out in shock that someone could be so insensitive, and just hugged her back. I'm sure in some way she meant well, but it sure put a damper on things that day. If more Snickers were the solution, I would have been back to my old self months ago. It was clear to me that chocolate couldn't solve this problem. Thankfully God could.

The next day I dropped the girls at church, and ran errands. But first I was able to sit with one of the Lisas. She was a big encouragement that day. I bet she didn't even realize how much so. I was also able to speak with the other Lisa's husband, Gary. I let him know that he was going to be called on to help my husband walk through this. He had been there as a husband. His wife, Lisa, had survived a brain tumor years before. I knew we would be covered in prayer while we traveled. That was such a comfort.

Then I went home and packed and packed some more. I was actually feeling somewhat functional. All the folding and packing left some thinking time though. Of all things running through my head, fear of death was not one of them. As you may recall, I saw Jesus in the shower. That's more than enough to wipe out any fear of death itself. It even left me with a twinge of excitement about what's to come.

Dying? Well that's another story. The dying part sounded horrific. As much as I didn't want to suffer through treatments that would likely only prolong the inevitable, I owed it to my kids and husband to at least try. So I resolved that day as I ran around, and packed like a madwoman, that I would do whatever I had to do. Even if that only meant dragging it out and causing more suffering, I would do it. I knew what was waiting for me when my life here ended. Nothing to fear. I just had to get there. But first: vacation. Buffers are wonderful things.

The next day arrived, and we had little to do except check and double check that we had everything we'd need. Our flight wasn't leaving until the early evening, so we weren't rushed to get out. A friend drove us up to Boston. When we got to the airport we met up with the rest of the family. We were all very excited, although my appearance was a bit disturbing to those who hadn't seen me in a while. We had a flight that would have us arriving in Shannon early the next morning. Our bodies would say it was the middle of the night...so it was going to be a long day. We watched a movie on the flight, and tried to snooze a little, but I don't think anyone got much actual sleep.

Everyone was excited when we got to Ireland. My sister's good friend, Billy, lives in Ireland and runs private tours. They were waiting for us when we arrived with a bus. The kids will tell you that the bus was one of the best parts of the trip. Lots of time for "cousining."

Since it was so early in the morning when we arrived, we weren't able to go to the hotel to check in just yet. Instead we drove over to The Cliffs of Mohr. Did I mention that it was raining? It was. And windy. It was very, very windy. It would have been miserable except I was on a tour bus in Ireland with a slew of people I loved dearly. We were all wet and tired, but we were having fun already.

After the visit there, we drove through some famous scenic area. I forgot what it was called. Probably because I missed it, as I was asleep on the bus. Most of us were asleep. Finally we made it to the hotel and were able to crash. Everyone did their own thing for dinner, but most napped first.

The jet lag kicked my butt. I was a zombie. But so was everyone else. Much of the beginning of the trip is a blur. The jet lag was rough, but when I adjusted to the time zone, I was so much closer to "normal" than I'd been in a while. I found myself walking the roads in the town where my great grandmother grew up over a hundred years earlier. She had left as a seventeen year old girl, and never returned to her home. It seemed kind of crazy that her great granddaughter was now walking the streets with some of her great-great grandchildren. I was doing so without the need to rest my hand on someone to keep my balance. I didn't need to stop every few minutes. I just keep walking!

We also stopped in a small village where my great -great grandparents had been born, and raised their family. It felt surreal to be walking the streets of the town that I had heard about from my Aunt Kit for years. She never made it to see the little town about which we all heard so much, but here I was.

Once the initial jet lag became manageable, I was amazingly functional. I was pretty impressed with myself. While I was vividly cognizant of what was ahead of us, I was able to just be in the moment. For the most part I didn't even think too much about what would happen when we got home. John sometimes had a funny look on his face when I caught him looking at me, but besides that he seemed to be doing just as well as I was.

We spent time in Cobh, and I was able to walk around and make my way through the Titanic museum. We also saw the remains of the dock that my ancestors would have used to travel to the US all those years ago. From there we went on to Waterford. I just kept getting more and more impressed with myself.

The days in Ireland went quickly. I tried to take things easy as much as possible. Often everyone would go to the pub in the hotel, and I would go up to the room with. Olivia. I probably could have pushed myself more than I did, but I thought I should take it easy like the doctor ordered. Once I adapted to the time change I was doing remarkably well. I was getting excited to see London for a few days.

In Dublin we ended the bus tour and stayed for several days. I was so encouraged that I managed to walk around the zoo, and take in other sights in the area. I was really impressing myself. It was a great end to an amazing family vacation. The anniversary part of the trip was ending, but we were heading to London to top off the vacation.

In England things looked somehow less grand than I'd expected. We managed to squeeze as much into the 3 days as possible. The Tower of London, The Tower Bridge, Big Ben, Buckingham Palace, Westminster Abbey, a River ride down the Thames, The London Eye.... It all kept my mind busy, but as the days progressed I knew it was getting to be time to face the music. We had to go back. Part of me couldn't wait to get out of London. There was something about the city that made it feel God-less. You could feel the spiritual darkness. It creeped me out, and it wasn't good timing to be creeped out. That made going home to face the music a little easier. I was ready to sleep in my own bed. We had the great family vacation. I got to spend a week with my parents, siblings, nieces, nephews, not to mention my own kids and husband. A dream come true. They'd all have a good memory when I was gone.

Chapter 8: Back to Reality. Wait, What?

I was ready now and just wanted it done. I knew I had only to wait until Monday afternoon to know what the next steps were going to be. I wanted to get on with it, and know what to expect.

We got home on Saturday. We were still on England time, so we were wide awake at 5am, and ready to get going to church. Church, of course, doesn't start at 5 am so we had a slow start to the morning. It was a nice change of pace to be home, and not rushing.

It was fabulous to sleep in my own bed, but I also knew what that privilege meant. It was time to deal with reality. I was starting to miss my buffer. Dealing with reality didn't sound nearly as fun as exploring Ireland and London with my family. As luck would have it, I had a Sunday morning before I had to deal with reality. The Holy Spirit could be my buffer. In fact when He's around, I don't even need the buffer. I could just let His peace deal with all the what ifs.

I don't really remember much about church that day. Just that it was good to be home, even if that meant reality was looming. It felt right to be back in church before the drama began the next day. The plan was for me to go alone to the appointment. Since all the bombs had already been dropped, all I was expecting was to make appointments for more tests and specialists. His office was supposed to deal with the insurance company while I was gone, so when I returned we'd be good to go. Let the tumor hunt begin!

The next morning I woke up to a spiritual high. It was truly strange from a completely rational and objective point of view. Why was I feeling so joyful? I had no illusions as to what the doctor's appointment later that day would mean. The process would be underway to find and deal with the cancer. So why am I feeling so joyful?

Jeremy Camp's song "Capture Me" had me dancing in the kitchen that morning. Interesting that He used Jeremy Camp's "I Still Believe" just a few weeks earlier to prepare my heart for the news I was about to get about the lab results. Perhaps He was preparing my heart again. But this time I wasn't sitting in my car crying. Instead, I was lifting my hands, swaying and dancing in my kitchen. All I could do was worship Him. Nothing else made sense.

Why wasn't I scared? I should have been. The buffer of a European vacation was gone. Reality loomed, and there I was dancing in the kitchen worshiping God. I felt like I was walking on a cloud all morning. Either the jet lag had me off my rocker, or God was holding me up and dancing with me.

He did a good job preparing my heart for the cancer battle I thought was before me. I wasn't prepared for what was actually about to happen at the appointment, though. It started with me running into my ninth grade English teacher in the waiting room. That was a pleasant surprise. When I was taken to the back I was happy to see I had gained a few pounds over the vacation. I was also surprised about that. As sweet as the Irish people are, the food was bland, bland, bland. I ate it though, and surprise! It was actually sticking to my ribs for once. This appointment was already starting out better than I had anticipated.

When the doctor came into the examination room, he didn't waste any time with pleasantries. He simply told me, "Your lab work no longer shows malignancy." Not what I was expecting. I was flabbergasted, and I'm sure my face showed my confusion

He went on to explain that his partner was very angry with him when he told her about my case. She was angry because he should not have let me go away. My labs were that bad. My cortisol levels were 5 times the outer edges of normal, and three times the level that indicates the presence of tumors, most likely cancerous tumors. No wonder his partner was angry. I was glad I didn't have this information before the trip. I knew I was obviously very sick, but wow. The perspective kind of blew me away, and made me understand why he was so insistent about the unlikelihood of a benign tumor causing the results.

He then apologized for being so frank with me in the last appointment, but he felt as though "I could handle it." That had to have been the Holy Spirit shining through, because if he could have seen me crying in the car before the appointment, he probably would have had a different opinion. Despite his apology, he once again went straight back into "telling it like it is" mode.

According to him, the new test results "Couldn't be right. It's just not possible." My "not consistent with malignancy" happy bubble was getting a little deflated.

When he said it wasn't possible to have these results, I may have irritated him by mentioning people praying for me. Clearly he was not a fan of divine intervention stealing his show. It was quickly decided that the labs would be rerun, and I wouldn't mention seeing Jesus in the shower.

So I was left with the knowledge that my lab results, which as it turns out were worse than I could have imagined, had inexplicably changed from a death sentence to normal. Obviously the new result was wrong according to the doctor. The original results showed cause for major concern on a number of fronts. He would rerun the labs, consult with some other doctors, and I would return when the results were in to decide how to proceed. He didn't offer much encouragement. He still strongly felt that cancer was the most likely possibility. We just needed some more evidence to get the health insurance on board with all the expensive diagnostics.

I had no idea what to think. A big part of me wanted to jump for joy, and high- five Jesus. The other part thought I should try to keep in touch with the very real possibility that I wasn't out of the woods yet. The doctor was pretty clear. He still thought I had cancer.

To say the visit was anticlimactic would be an understatement. I came ready to start the battle, and left wondering if the battle might be over. The doctor didn't think things were over, he was clear about that. But then there was the other evidence. I was starting to gain weight, I could walk across a room without having to steady myself, I wasn't covered in disturbing bruises anymore, and the fatigue was at bay. I was no longer feeling sickly. Tired? Sure, but I was a homeschooling mother of 3, of course I was tired.

John and I approached the unexpected turn of events with cautious optimism. We knew the next visit could put us right back where we were, but we decided to just carry on with all that needed to be done. That would be the start of the school year. It didn't look like anything was going to change with school in the near future. Rachel was starting high school in a few days. So much to get done. Olivia was playing soccer, and Alex was playing fall ball. We were busy. That didn't leave much time for thinking and worrying.

Meanwhile I noticed a curious thing. After months of trying to gain weight, and still losing, I was gaining weight all of a sudden. I want to be clear here: neither the weight loss, nor weight gain was under my control. While desperately trying to gain weight during the spring and summer I was met only with weight loss. This sometimes led to "helpful tips" to help me gain weight. Now I was gaining. That wasn't my doing either. I was eating normal. The same diet that had me losing weight for months now had me gaining weight. Clearly it wasn't my doing. I was pretty sure it was God's doing. It's the only thing that made sense.

We were so busy that the time went quickly, and before I knew it we were one day away from the return visit. Would everything change again?

We decided on the spur of the moment to go apple picking after church that Sunday. This was a big move on my part. I was in long skirt, and high heel boots. Would I be able to pull this off? Walking though church without feeling faint was one thing, but apple picking in high heels? That sounded risky.

We had a great time. Despite looking fashionable in my boots, I managed to walk around the orchard without once feeling lightheaded or tripping. I didn't know what the doctor would say the next day, but one thing I knew without a doubt: I was a different person than I was a month ago. A month before being told that I had cancer made perfect sense. I was clearly a very sick woman. Now here I was apple picking in fabulous boots, and not falling down. I was even starting to look a little better. I had gained some weight, and although people would still randomly, and accusingly tell me to put on some weight, they no longer added, "You look terrible." Progress.

If I thought the last doctor's visit was unexpected and strange, I was in for yet more bewilderment. You would think he would be pleased to see the progress I was making. That wasn't the case. He was furious, or at least seemed to be pretty angry with me. He came into the exam room and told me that the results were the same as last time. They were no longer showing malignancy. He actually seemed very upset with me, as though I was pulling a scam on him. He angrily informed me, that he had already sent a letter to my doctor telling her about my poor prognosis. He appeared more upset that he would have to retract the prognosis, than by the idea of a mother dying a painful death. Pride can be a fragile thing for a doctor.

He went on to tell me that the other doctors he consulted with agreed that the results were now normal. And that's when it got really weird. Any remnants of the apologetic, concerned doctor I met at the last two visits disappeared. He was replaced with a prideful, angry mess of a man. I innocently asked what he thought could have caused the abnormal results. I knew better than to mention God's hand in all this. He was angry enough, without me pointing out that he's not God.

He then went on to quite angrily and with much hostility tell me that I obviously had some deeply buried anxiety and depression, perhaps a repressed memory, that had caused the abnormal results. I needed to get counseling so they could "dig deep" and bring to the surface whatever my issue was. He had no answer as to how the results could have turned normal. There hadn't been any deep digging yet, and now my results were normal.

I was more confused than ever. I foolishly explained that I didn't seem to have any symptoms of depression or anxiety. This further angered him, while he listed off symptoms that he claimed I had, although he never asked about them. Apparently I had lost interest in things I used to enjoy. I was not aware of this, but somehow he was. Yes, it was bizarre. I didn't dare tell him about seeing Jesus in the shower. That might have thrown him over the edge.

He decided that I should have one more blood test where I would have to take a prescription before bed, and have blood drawn in the morning. If the results on that were fine then we could conclude that I didn't have tumors, but was in fact suffering from some unknown mental illness. He couldn't get me out of the office fast enough. In fact I had to call out to him while I was checking out to see if he wanted me to make a follow up appointment. It was without a doubt the strangest appointment of my life.

I truly didn't know what to think. On the surface it seemed like cause for celebration. Another "no sign of malignancy" report. I should be jumping for joy. His anger and hostility left me a bit flabbergasted however. I wanted to be happy about the news, and I'm feeling better after all these months, but this was just so strange. Do we celebrate? Am I cancer free, but maybe a little bit crazy? Or maybe he was the crazy one. He was clearly upset that my labs no longer showed cancer, which seemed a bit off to me. But what do I know? According to him there's a good chance I'm completely unaware of what's going on in my own life. I'm not sure how my buried angst caused my body to not absorb nutrients, though. Cause I know for a fact that I was eating plenty of food. Maybe when you're carrying around a deeply buried emotional trauma your body decides to stop absorbing nutrition and breaks out in bruises as a clue. It didn't seem plausible. And his Jekyll and Hyde persona made me doubt his wisdom in anything. It was a puzzle, but we'd just wait on the newest round of blood work and in the meantime carry on. Who knows, maybe I had been abducted by aliens as a child.

We did tell the kids at this point what had happened. They were pleased to hear I no longer appeared to be dying. A few months later when I asked each of them what they were thinking while I was sick, I learned I hadn't fooled anyone. All three admitted they thought I was probably dying in the midst of it all.

Since I was feeling better I decided to try exercising again. I had quit exercising on the stationary bike we have because it made me too dizzy. I just couldn't pull it off without hurting myself. But things were changing, and now I could exercise like a normal person. It felt good! I was me again....except for the haunting fear that I may have some dark secret that my mind was covering up. OK, I really wasn't afraid of that. I thought perhaps he was the one with some childhood trauma. That could explain the Jekyll and Hyde persona.

Throughout that week God continued to stalk me with Mercyme's "The Hurt and the Healer" song. I guess He wanted to make sure I understood what He had been up to these past few months.

"So here I am

What's left of me

Where glory meets my suffering

I'm alive

Even though a part of me has died

You take my heart and breathe it back to life

I fall into Your arms open wide

When the hurt and the healer collide"[6]

Now the way God had stalking me with this song was making more and more sense. If the newest labs were right, and the preponderance of evidence was looked at objectively, it would appear that He healed me.

But there where parts I still didn't understand. It didn't make sense that "a part of me had died." If anything I had come alive in new ways. Even though I didn't know what He meant, I was willing to fall into His arms. He'd never failed me before. So I did just that.

A few days later the doctor, aka Jekyll and Hyde, called. He reported that the labs were normal. I then asked if there was a next step. This got him angry again. The man was a ticking time bomb. To him, me and my hope filled attitude was the problem.

I started to ask him another question. At this point he yelled at me like I was naughty child. He was very upset that I supposedly interrupted him. So I remained silent, as did he. After a few seconds of awkward silence I again attempted to ask a question, but this time I first asked if he was done speaking. He hadn't said anything since I attempted to speak, and he screamed at me. This time he was no more helpful. I asked why he would tell me I had cancer if the results could indicate depression. He never screened me for any mental health issues. This again infuriated him. I thought it was a logical question. He disliked the fact that I was asking logical questions instead of bowing to the God-like self-image he was carrying around.

It became very clear he had no intention of answering any of my questions in a helpful manner. At that point I told him that I would follow up with my general practitioner, and ended the painful call. I really had no new information except for the fact that the doctor was prideful beyond compare, and quite frankly a jackass. But I kind of knew that from the last office visit. The fact that God was the one who had saved me and not him was just too much for his ego. It seems he would have preferred for me to accommodate his massive ego with a tumor. For now, I was done with him.

Chapter 9: Confirmations

When I hung up, I called my GP, and made an appointment for the next day. I was beyond bewildered at this point. I had moved on to flummoxed. Despite my confused state, I was clearly getting better, day by day. My weight continued to increase. I could not only walk around without growing faint, but I could also exercise. It was like I was back to normal. There was something that had changed, but I couldn't really put my finger on it. It was a good change, though, so I wouldn't waste energy trying to figure it out.

At the doctor's office it was confirmed that I had gained back more than half of the weight I had lost. I didn't look the part of the dying waif that I had been projecting for the past few months. She, too, was surprised by the story I told of my recent visit and phone call with the Endocrinologist. Unlike Dr. Jekyll she was happy to see the improvements.

She was able to do the impossible: get me an appointment with a different endocrinologist later that week. Ironically I had made and canceled an appointment with this same doctor. At the time I had made the appointment originally, it was a several months wait. But my doctor called him, and they managed to squeeze me in on a few days' notice.

At this point I wasn't looking to learn what was wrong, so much as to confirm that the labs were in fact normal. I wasn't feeling like Jekyll/Hyde could be trusted. I fully expected this new doctor to say things looked good, because...well...things were looking good. I still had some weight to gain back, but that was happening without me even trying. And I could walk around now, and wear boots, and even kitchen dance. I was back!

As expected, the new endocrinologist confirmed that I no longer appeared to be dying. The last two rounds of labs were normal. He was taken aback by the earlier results. He confirmed that they indicated cancer, or at least tumors secreting cortisol into my bloodstream. He wondered aloud how the results could have changed so dramatically. So I told him. I didn't mention seeing Jesus in the shower. I'm not sure how he would have taken that information. He didn't really say anything when I told him my, "God healed me theory." He just smiled and nodded.

It did occur to me that most people suffering from repressed traumatic depressive disorders (yeah, I think I just made that term up), might not be aware of the problem. So I asked him if it was possible that the results could have been caused by depression or anxiety. He actually chuckled. Adrenal levels can be elevated in depression, but not to that extent. Somewhat elevated, not off the charts elevated. My levels were five times removed from normal. It was cancer territory, not abducted by aliens in a former life territory.

Just to be responsible, he ordered yet another round of blood tests. He had me make a follow up appointment, and I was off. I felt good. I was looking pretty normal, feeling pretty normal...and I had confirmation that the lab results were normal. Now that I knew that I probably hadn't been abducted by aliens, and I was no longer dying I was ready to get on with things.

Which was good, very good. If you've ever been a homeschooling mother of 3 in the fall, you know there really is no time to be sick, or feel fatigued. Way too much to get done. There was school, and baseball, and soccer, and homeschool classes, field trips...and on and on. My church had the women's retreat coming up the next month, and I was the director.

It was a strange time. More shocking than how sick I had gotten was how fast I shot back up. Weight that took six months to fall away was gained back in a matter of weeks without any change in my eating habits or diet. It was crazy! I could walk around without concern, and I could even exercise. Everything was just about back to normal it seemed, except for one thing. I couldn't put my finger on what that thing was though.

About a week later I was in the grocery store when I got a call from the new Endocrinologist on my cell. He reported that all the labs had come back normal. The doctor reiterated that he couldn't explain how my labs had changed so dramatically, but he didn't see any reason for me to come back to see him unless something changed. He would be in touch with my doctor, but there was nothing more he had to add.

That left me with the strange reality that I had apparently been healed. I just didn't know exactly what it was that He healed me from. I had pretty good idea, but no exact answer to the question. People would ask, and I didn't really have an answer for them. All I could tell them was that He had healed me.

Around this time, I started enjoying some time with God in the mornings out on my deck before school started for the day. The leaves were starting to turn and God's glory was a beautiful way to start each day. So on this particular morning, I asked God what the deal was. Did he heal me? Because it seemed like quite a few people prayed for healing for me, or so I thought, but when He healed me many of those same people didn't, believe He could have actually pulled it off. I thought He could, and I thought He did, but it didn't hurt to ask. He's used to all my questions by now.

So I asked my question, and flipped open my Bible. I landed in John 9. John 9 tells the story of the man born blind who Jesus heals. The poor man is healed and sees for the first time, and is then hammered by the unbelief all around him. As the questioning and accusations continue he replies, "Whether he is a sinner or not, I do not know. One thing I do know, I was blind but now I see."

Of course this is the story God put in front of me that morning. I was getting so discouraged by the unbelief all around me. Time and time again someone would ask me what I thought "really happened." These were the very people who I thought were praying for healing for me. I found the question confusing. But God wasn't confused by it. He answered my question about the healing, but He also showed me that I shouldn't be discouraged by the unbelief of others. Even while He walked the Earth and healed in people's sight, they didn't believe. I shouldn't be discouraged to see so much of the same in our day. I should expect it.

He also directed me to the story of Peter's miraculous escape from prison in Acts 12. The early church was gathered in prayer for Peter's release. When God answered their prayer miraculously, they didn't believe it was possible. In fact they believed so strongly that Peter couldn't be at the door, that they told the servant girl that she was out of her mind. The poor girl must have been so frustrated by their unbelief. I knew the feeling.

God was quick to point out to me that people are given different spiritual gifts. One of mine is faith, so believing God comes easier for me. I shouldn't have been so discouraged by the unbelief around me. At this time I was so Christ-focused that I was able to agree and move on. As a side note: God is always right. You can save time and angst if you just go with that from the start.

I had so much going on during this time frame, and things were coming at me quickly. Before I knew it, it was time for our church's fall women's retreat. As the leader of the women's ministry team, that was my gig. Thankfully so many women had stepped forward during the summer while I was sick and we were planning the retreat that it wasn't nearly the stress inducing event you might imagine.

When the retreat came, everything went off without a hitch. During one of the retreat sessions we were led through some "quiet time" activities as we moved from station to station reflecting on different aspects of our relationship with God. At one of the stations the question was posed in the retreat journal: What are the dark valleys you're facing in your life? What doubts are nagging at you?

So I wrote in the journal: Is the healing complete? Is there anything else wrong, or am I really OK? Am I doing enough for my family?"

A few minutes later I got a text from Jesus. Technically it was from John, but it was a direct answer to the question I had just asked God. In the text he told me that I had gotten a letter from my doctor about my recent lab work, and all the results were completely normal. The text didn't say anything in answer to my question about my family, but it took care of the other question pretty well.

I had in the past suggested that He use email or text to answer some of my endless questions. I'm in the habit of offering God my suggestions for a better running of the universe, you see. Usually He handles it just fine without my help, but it was fun to see that He took my recommendation in this case. I was fine, and could continue on in the confidence only He gives.

The following weekend I was off to a Chris Tomlin concert with some homeschool mommy friends. It was such a fun night. We took a van to Lowell, Massachusetts, where we may or may not have stalked his bus.

It was such a normal thing to do. Maybe not so much the stalking his bus part, but the rest was normal. I was so thankful for the turn my life took when I dropped to my knees all those weeks ago. I went from dead girl walking, to an alive girl dancing. Chris Tomlin introduced a new song that would be on the album that was due out in a few weeks. God was speaking directly to me, and blessing my confidence in Him.

"I know who goes before me

I know who stands behind

The God of angel armies

Is always by my side

The one who reigns forever

He is a friend of mine

The God of angel armies

Is always by my side"[7]

Oh, boy! Did I love praising God that night! Life was moving on, and it was good. So good, in so many ways. I bought the single of Chris' newest song, and pre-ordered the cd which was due out in a few weeks. It was a fun night, and I really was back to normal life. I finally figured out what "that thing" that was different about how I felt. I did feel back to normal in every way except one, everything was better than it had been before. That was what was different. We were happy before and during, and we were happier now than when it had started.

A few days after the concert, I went back to my doctor for a follow up appointment. By this time my weight was just a few pounds from my weight when it all began. I was feeling good, and my labs were all good. At one point she asked if she could ask me a question. I told her, "Sure."

"You were a very sick woman."

"Yes, I know. I felt like a very sick woman."

"No, I don't mean your symptoms, or how you felt. I'm talking about your lab work. You were a very sick woman. We didn't do anything, and now look at you. You gained the weight back, your labs are all normal. What do you think happened?"

Well, that certainly left the door wide open. Perhaps this is part of what He meant all those months ago when He said He would show Himself to others through the trial I was about to experience. So I told her that I thought had happened. I probably did have cancer somewhere, and God healed me. It was the only thing that made sense when I pieced the months together.

She smiled, shook her head a bit, and said, "Well, that's as a good an explanation as I can come up with." It seemed everyone was in agreement that the health crisis was over. I could get back to living.

Not long before Thanksgiving that year, I was contacted by a young mom I know who wanted someone, a

Christian woman, to talk through a few things in her life. We met for coffee, and had a good time together. It felt good to feel useful again. I was being used through the retreat, and Bible study, but I didn't have much room for personal one on one ministry. It felt right to be used to speak into someone's life again. The feeling was short lived.

Around this time, I shared parts of this testimony with someone else, and it wasn't well received. At all. Besides that, there were quite a few "believers" who seemed more comfortable believing that all the tests were wrong and my symptoms disappearing was just a convenient coincidence, than in believing God healed me. I was running low on conviction to tell my story. I knew what happened, maybe that was all that mattered. Maybe what happened was supposed to just stay between God and my family.

He even filled me in on why it had to get so bad before it got better. I wouldn't have known what He had done if it hadn't gotten so bad. And then there was the fact that I hadn't asked. Not that He was being legalistic, but that He was letting me be a part of it. It took me so long to just ask knowing He could. But when I did, He pulled me out of the pit. Even knowing this, I don't regret not asking sooner. If I had I would have missed out on some of the blessings along the way. They were worth the hard times. Plus, God had brought so much good from it all. Everything in my life seemed a little better.

Before I knew it we were heading into the Christmas season. I'm blessed with a husband who is actually very useful during the holiday season. He'll do a great deal of shopping, and helps keep track of all the things that have to be dealt with during that time. Time was moving along, and the summer was fading a bit. The busyness of life took over. That Christmas everything seemed a little better as well. I decided to live dangerously and go easy on all the lists. This was unprecedented, but fun. The only real list I made was a shopping list for breakfast on Christmas morning, and then I proceeded to leave the list at home.   I was pretty proud that I didn't forget a thing.

It was a great Christmas. I was going with the flow and everything was perfect. The fact that I was still there with my family, and not in the hospital or in heaven made it all the sweeter.

Chapter 10: The Thorn Appears

Sometimes I get busy, and lose sight of things. It can happen without me even noticing. We made it through Christmas, and were on to the New Year. Before I knew it, I was moving on to a new attitude. Not a good one. I was pretty sure that most of the world might be in a conspiracy against me. This might be a good time to mention that I was apparently having some hormonal issues. I was not digging things at all. I was pretty sure that everyone else I came in contact with was probably an idiot, or mean. Maybe both.

I was pretty miserable. The after Christmas lull gave my mind time to wander, and it didn't wander to good places. Instead it wandered to places of hurt and even anger. It's funny how God let's me go off on my little tangents at times before He reels me back in.

I have to say, I was very hurt and very angry. All the potential hurts from months before were being brought to my mind. At the time that things happened my reality was Jesus waiting for me. Remember the shower? I didn't let myself dwell on the hurts while it was happening. But now I was months removed. I wasn't dead, and I could be outraged.

I'm going to assume that people weren't being intentionally cruel. But there were people who approached me with judgment rather than concern. My weight loss was cause for disdain rather than compassion for quite a few. I really don't know why that was. I would think a dim-witted monkey could have figured out I was sick. Especially if the monkey could read. I didn't keep the struggle a secret. I repeatedly asked for prayer about the unexplained weight loss. Instead of compassion, I mostly met condemnation. In the eyes of some, it seems, my weight loss was my own fault. When the fatigue kicked in, and I was finding walking around a challenge, I was told to "eat more." No one offered any practical help to my family, just words of wisdom that hurt more than they helped.

As it turns out, there are a whole lot of Christians who pray not believing. I was shocked by the number of "believers" who couldn't wrap their minds around the obvious. God had healed me. From what exactly, I don't know. It was so strange to me that unbelievers, like my doctor, could see that something extraordinary had happened. But the very people who were praying for me didn't see it. It still makes me wonder what they were praying for, or what they were expecting. Clearly healing was not what they had in mind.

God did point out to me again that my spiritual gifts, one of which is faith, are not the same gifts everyone is given. Even so, I did find it strange and bewildering. And very hurtful. It was the same delightful folks who wanted me to always know how badly I looked who couldn't grasp that God can and does heal. I feel badly for those people now. At the time I was just mad, though. I may have suggested repeatedly that God smack these folks upside the head. He's much nicer than me, so I don't know that he took my advice.

While I was sick, I managed to let most of it roll off my back. I had little choice. I was dying, and I knew it. My focus had to be on my family for what time I had left. But when it was all over, I let the hurt envelope me. And the anger. I was so angry.

Now, I want to stop here and clarify that there were people, mostly my brothers and sisters in Christ, who I knew had my back. They did care, and were faithful to lift me up in prayer. God used that knowing to sustain me during some difficult hours.

But boy, did I let God have it a few times. I was mostly venting about hurtful things said to me, and the lack of help offered to us. I was mad, so I often gave God an earful. He was very patient, but He also let me know when I had pushed it too far.

I once lamented to Him that I had poured my life out for these people. Where were they when I needed help? He actually seemed to use sarcasm with me. He said, "You poured your life out for them? I thought you did those things for me." The tone of voice was clear. He was not impressed with my whining.

That kind of left me face to face with a dilemma. Who had I poured my life out for? Was it for Christ, or for the people He put before me? If it's Christ, why am I complaining about pouring my life out? He went a little further than me in the "pouring your life out" department, I think. I was fully cognizant of the fact that I should stop my whining. I wasn't done yet. Now and then He lets me have my moment of complaining, but He specializes in reeling me back in. Good thing. I'd hate to see where I'd be without Him always taking me back.

Beyond that, things were good on the surface. We were all doing fine, except my hormonal tendencies. I knew I was dealing with a "thorn." Perhaps it was in some way related to the thorn in Paul's side. But He pushed through, and I was determined to do the same. Push through.

One of the best ways I know to push through is to kitchen dance. I suppose any form of worship would work, but I liked to praise God in my kitchen with song and dance. He really doesn't seem to mind. The rest of the family sometimes does mind, but God seems cool with it. I'd just put on worship songs and dance as I did whatever chores needed to be done. Sometimes I skipped the chores and just danced. This is probably what kept me together those few months.

The Chris Tomlin CD arrived and I discovered the song, "God's Great Dance Floor." I was sure he wrote it about my kitchen. Although I could praise Him every day, I was spending too much time looking back. I wasn't looking back at all He had done for me. Instead I was looking at what I thought others had done to me. It wasn't healthy. I knew it wasn't, but a part of me wanted to be allowed to wallow in my misery for a while.

Even with all of the kitchen dancing, I was still clinging to my anger and hurt. At one point a friend who I hadn't heard from in months called. The last she heard I was getting the labs rerun months earlier. I was happy to hear from her at first. She was calling to ask how I was doing. I wish she had left it at that. She didn't. She went on to tell me that she was embarrassed because her family was asking how I was doing and she didn't know. It was better when I could have talked myself into thinking she cared, despite the month's long silence. But that wasn't the case, and her lack of concern was probably one of the biggest hurts in all of it. It seemed as if the hurts kept piling up.

As angry as I was, I knew I obviously had some medical issue. My hormones where wound way too tight. I had to be deal with that. I had an appointment coming up for my annual in a month....so I waited. In the meantime I tried to control the Rolodex in my brain. All the hurts were stinging, as if they were new. Most of the hurtful things had happened months ago. I let it go then. Why couldn't I just let it go now?

Chapter 11: Two by Fours

I have to say He is very patient, but at the same time tells it like it is. One day I was telling on all the people who didn't offer to help us. You know, just in case He didn't know already. In His gentle, yet sarcastic way, He asked: "Who did you ask to help you that didn't help?" He did have point. Apart from asking for women to help with planning the retreat, and women's ministry events, I really hadn't asked for help. When I did ask for help with church stuff people showed up big time.

Apart from church, I hadn't actually asked anyone for help. In many ways I didn't think I needed help at the time. I could just keep pushing through, and John was doing a pretty good job keeping things running. He was the one that probably could have used a hand. At any rate, God had me there. I hadn't asked, and we managed to get through it without help. Why was I whining about this now, months later?

One day I was in full "complain to the God of the universe" mode. I truly don't know how He puts up with me and continues to pour out mercy on me every day. As you may have gathered, I can be a real pain. As I was scrolling through Facebook I noticed a status update from a former schoolmate who had cancer. He was commenting that he had survived 6 months, even though the doctors didn't expect him to make it that long. 6 months? Wait a minute...

When I saw the post, I clicked over to a support page for him that I had been following. I noticed the date of his diagnosis. It was the day after the appointment when I was first told that the labs had changed and didn't show cancer anymore. So the day after I was told that the lab results changed from death sentence, to maybe not, he was being told the opposite. I hadn't noticed that before. It was an odd coincidence.

As I'm sitting at the computer desk pondering this, my phone rings. It was my mother. She was calling to tell me that my aunt, who had been diagnosed with cancer around the same time as I was going through all the struggles that summer, had died somewhat unexpectedly that day. It was practically a physical two by four coming down to shake me up. It worked. I was shook up.

I knew I was being a brat. When I was at the foot of the cross, He was all I could see. Here's the thing: He didn't go anywhere, I did. At the very least I looked away. I stopped looking at the wonder of my savior, the miracle of His healing in my life, and all He'd done for me. Instead I looked at all I thought I had to get done, and rehashed all the hurts from the past year. How that is possible, I do not know. But I did. I looked away, and tried paddling through life on my own power again. Big mistake. I was going nowhere, fast. Still He was there, waiting for me to get over myself and throw myself at His mercy again. As my maker, He knows me pretty well. He knew how to speak to me; I just had to learn to listen again.

Everything seemed to be one big deja vu. A year before in that very month my grandmother had died. That was when I first realized I was shrinking. I would be going up to the same area, with the same relatives for this funeral. At the funeral I learned that my aunt's cancer ordeal had started 6 months earlier with a blood test result that indicated cancer somewhere. This would have been happening at the same time I was hearing the same news about my test results. In her case, they found the cancer in her lungs. In my case it "went away."

On the off chance I needed a bigger two by four to wake me up, I was asked to do a reading at the funeral Mass. As I'm standing there reading from God's word, God was telling me, "Look at what I did for you. Look!"

Before me was a casket holding my aunt. Six months earlier we both received the same news about our lab results from the doctor. She's lying in a casket, and I'm standing here, healthy, reading from His word at her funeral. I don't think He could have been clearer about my brattiness. He is so full of mercy, and I just take it for granted.

When I returned home from the funeral we had a Game Show Night at our church. We were team leaders. It did occur to me that the weekend after my grandmother's funeral the year before was also a Game Show Night where we were leading a team. It was getting pretty weird. The deja vu wake up was very effective. I was now fully aware of what a brat I had been. I clearly needed to get my eyes back where they belonged.

I remember one afternoon in particular. I had dropped my two youngest at Boy Scouts and Heritage Girls. I was running errands, and letting my mental Rolodex take a little spin. I had just told God, out loud, that I didn't even know who I was anymore. Without skipping a beat the next song on the radio started playing. Within a few notes, I recognized the song and began to laugh. It was Jason Gray singing, "Remind Me Who I Am." You should go listen to it right now.

"When I lose my way,

And I forget my name,

Remind me who I am.

In the mirror all I see,

Is who I don't wanna be,

Remind me who I am.

In the loneliest places,

When I can't remember what grace is.

Tell me once again who I am to You,

Who I am to You.

Tell me lest I forget who I am to You,

That I belong to You.

To You.

When my heart is like a stone,

And I'm running far from home,

Remind me who I am.

When I can't receive Your love,

Afraid I'll never be enough,

Remind me who I am.

If I'm Your beloved,

Can You help me believe it."[8]

The way he was always whipping out the right song at exactly the right moment delights and amuses me. In this case He was teasing me a little. Sometimes I need a little sarcasm, and sometimes I need God to tease me. But He's faithful to let me know when I'm being ridiculous.

It was getting to be time for the Spring Bible studies to be decided. One of my team members had suggested Unglued: Making Wise Choices in the Midst of Raw Emotions, by Lysa Terkeurst. After meeting with the pastor, and praying about the upcoming studies I felt that God really wanted us to use Unglued with the ladies. This time I wasn't as naïve as I had been the year before with the "Brave" study. I knew He was talking about me, and I was ready for it. Or at least I wanted to be ready for it.

God had my attention, but there was still the issue of the thorn to deal with. It was decided at my annual that the physical stress of the past year had taken a toll. My body had shut down in some areas, and the revving up to get back to normal was probably the cause of some of my issues. She decided to schedule me for an ultrasound and to see what was going on. The earliest I could get was about 5 weeks out. That was good; I had too many things to get done. I'd deal with that when I had the time.

Meanwhile God was stalking me with Tenth Avenue North songs again. "Worn" could have been my anthem. I was no longer physically worn, but I was worn in a number of ways.

"Let me see redemption win

Let me know the struggle ends

That you can mend a heart

That's frail and torn

I wanna know a song can rise

From the ashes of a broken life

And all that's dead inside can be reborn

Cause I'm worn"[9]

My heart was frail and torn in so many ways. I so wanted to let it go, and move on with life. I really did. I just didn't know how to do that. I could tell that God was on the case, though. Now that I was looking again, He was making Himself so clear.

Their song "Losing" was another wake up call for me. He wanted me to move on. I was being so stubborn. I was like an overtired 5 year old. I was going to stomp my feet, and refuse to let Him take it from me until I was done throwing my tantrum.

"I can't believe what she said

I can't believe what he did

Oh, don't they know it's wrong, yeah?

Don't they know it's wrong, yeah?

Maybe there's something I missed

But how could they treat me like this?

It's wearing out my heart

The way they disregard

This is love, this is hate...

We all have a choice to make

Oh, Father won't You forgive them?

They don't know what they've been doin' (oh no)

Oh, Father, give me grace to forgive them

'Cause I feel like the one losin'"[10]

This song summed up my struggle pretty well. In theory I wanted to forgive and move on...in theory. In reality, I was still hurt and angry. I would continue to wallow in it for a little longer. Because I was 100% sure that I was right. I was mistreated, I was deserted, I was uncared for, I was mad! And hurt. I just needed to move past the mad part. The hurt part had some value. I now knew who I could count on in a crisis. I was married to him. As much as it hurt to realize that some people wouldn't be there when I needed help, it was also freeing. In a strange way it's good to know who will have your back, even if that knowledge stings some.

It was good timing for God to stalk me with Tenth Avenue North music. You'd think He could preordain these things or something. They were coming to a church about an hour away. My oldest daughter was also a big fan. We bought tickets for a meet and greet with the band before the concert that included priority seating. I was very excited because, as I may have mentioned, I like to sing and dance and worship God.

We were going with one of the Lisas. She was the one who may or may not have yelled at the Lord of the universe when I was told I had tumors somewhere. Her daughter was a good friend of my daughter. Did I mention that Lisa had a brain tumor when she was pregnant with her now teen daughter? That may explain her yelling at God over my tumor situation. She knew what she was talking about. Of course I've been known to yell in His general direction over much less.

The concert was amazing. During the meet and greet I asked Mike Donehey, the lead singer, if he was ever freaked out to hear testimonies about how God used his songs. I then gave a very brief testimony about Hold My

Heart, and how God had used that song in my life. I probably could have given testimony about a number of songs, but they had a concert to put on for us.

Now I could be wrong about this, but I'm pretty sure Mike kept looking at me in the third row while he sang Hold My Heart later in the concert. My vision was blurred by tears, so I may be wrong, but it sure seemed like he kept looking right at me. Or maybe he was looking at the person behind me. Either way, the night was just one more confirmation that God was by my side, and He wasn't going anywhere.

Chapter 12: Letting Go

In the middle of some of my complaining days, John and I both had the same seemingly random conviction. We should really consider moving. Moving to Tennessee to be more specific. Which is even more random than it sounds because I've never even been in the state. At least John had been there. It made sense for a host of reasons, but mostly because it seemed to be God's idea to a large extent. From a financial standpoint it was a no brainer. We lived in a state with a very high tax burden. A move to Tennessee would likely save us ten thousand a year in taxes alone. The cost of living was so much less. College and the accompanying bills are looming in a few years. John's job was portable. He worked from home. He could do that anywhere. It made no sense to stay from that perspective.

I was worried about the effect of moving on the kids. One night I was in the shower again. This time Jesus wasn't there, but still He spoke. I was asking about this very thing. Moving five years ago seems like it would have been a better option. Why didn't He tell us to move then? Staying here was easier. We already knew how things worked, and I knew what homeschool hoops I had to jump through. I'd have to deal with a whole new set of hoops. The kids would be resistant to moving from their social lives and friends. I was filling God in on all this when He told me quite clearly, "It's for the kids."

He didn't have any more to say than that. I didn't really know what to make of it, except that He was definitely in the situation as much as I felt. John actually went down for a few days to do some initial scouting. It made so much sense. I still hadn't been, but I was on board with wherever He was leading. I had already discovered the previous summer that we could manage and be happy even if we were isolated from people. And with cell phones we wouldn't really be that isolated from our families. It was another good distraction, and gave the Rolodex a productive reason to spin. It seemed a little crazy, but I was up for an adventure. At least it had me looking forward expectantly rather looking back.

Around the same time, we were working through the Unglued study. It was very helpful. Turns out, God once again knew what He was doing. One night I was walking out to the parking lot at church with two friends. I'll call them Denise and Sharon since that's their names. They were encouraging me about how I had been struggling. I knew I had to do something about it. I was hoping the upcoming ultrasound would reveal something about why I seemed to be coming unglued.

As it turned out, God decided to beat the doctor to the punch. I got in my car and started it up to head home. I had a Tenth Avenue North CD in the player. The CD was my daughter's. We had been listening to it when we went up to the show the week earlier. The first song I heard was "By Your Side." He always gets me with this song! Every time

"Why are you striving these days?

Why are you trying to earn grace?

Why are you crying?

Let me lift up your face

Just don't turn away.

Why are you looking for love?

Why are you still searching

As if I'm not enough?

To where will you go child?

Tell me where will you run

To where will you run?

'Cause I'll be by your side wherever you fall,

In the dead of night whenever you call.

And please don't fight these hands that are holding you

My hands are holding you".[11]

God and I have very blunt and frank conversations, especially in the car. Even more so when I hear something that I don't want to hear, even though I really do want to hear it. Might seem confusing to follow, but God always gets it. So I gave Him my thoughts on the matter. "I know you're by my side God...I love that you're by my side...I know I need to stop fighting you, I just don't know what to do about all the bitterness that's growing in me. It's worse than the tumors, but I can't let it go!" Then the next song started. It was "Let It Go." You can't make this stuff up.

"I've been holding on so tight

Look at these knuckles they've gone white

I'm fighting for who I want to be

I'm just trying to find security

But you say let it go

You say let it go

You say life is waiting for the ones who lose control

You say You will be everything I need

You say if I lose my life it's then I'll find my soul

You say let it go"[12]

So I let Him have it. "I want to let it go, I've tried to let it go. I just can't do it! I can't! I give up. You've got to do it! I quit!"

"That's what I was waiting for," was His gentle response.

You would think I would have learned this by now. We've had the same conversation a number of times. It always ended the same way. I finally give up all of my prideful striving, throw it at His feet, and He moves mountains. Or in this case a thorn.

So I begged him, much like I had months earlier when I asked Him to "take it out of me." Last time it was tumors. This time it was the festering anger and bitterness that threatened me more than the tumors had. On the outside, I may have seemed OK, but on the inside I was a mess. I was losing my joy, and I wanted it back. I wanted to be me again. So I threw up my hands in defeat, and begged Him to do it for me. I probably should have done that's months earlier.

At some point the next day I realized the bitterness was gone. Missing in action. Nowhere to be found. I figured it could rear its ugly head again at any moment, but it didn't. It stayed away the next day too. Jesus spoke, and BOOM! It was gone. Again I don't know how He does these things. He just speaks them into being. If I hadn't experienced it myself, I wouldn't have believed it was possible. Removing the bitterness actually seemed a bigger miracle to me. I had no attachment to the tumors. The bitterness I seemed to enjoy in some strange way. Even though this miracle lacked the accompanying lab reports to confirm what had happened, it was all the more impressive to me.

First He saved my soul all those years ago. Next He saved my physical body, and now He had saved my spirit. The last two times, in particular, I was fading fast when He stepped in to bring me back. And all I had to do was ask Him. That was it. Believe Him, and throw myself at His mercy. Every time, same result. It's actually a pretty simple formula. It really should be my go-to position, not my fallback position. Maybe someday, I'll learn.

Chapter 13: The Thorn Revealed

When the appointment finally rolled around for the ultrasound, I was feeling pretty normal. No longer ruled by rogue hormones. The doctor was giving me the ultrasound when he said, "Here it is. Look at this." He sounded a wee bit excited.

He turned the screen, as I silently prayed, "Please no heartbeat, please no heartbeat."

Thankfully there was no heartbeat. There was a strange something hanging out in my uterus, though. The doctor explained it was a polyp. A thorn shaped polyp to be more precise. He actually remarked that it looked like a thorn. I laughed. He may have thought I was losing it. What's so funny about a thorn shaped polyp? You had to be in my head to see what was so funny about that, I guess. God does good work, especially when He's trying to get His point across to a stubborn woman.

All we needed to do now was get rid of the polyp. That involved a simple procedure at the hospital. Not a big deal at all. Except for the bill. The Affordable Care Act was costing us big time now. Ironically if there had been a heartbeat, basically the same procedure would have been covered in full. But since no one would die, the bill was over $8000 and our portion for an outpatient surgery was pretty hefty.

This financial blip would put on hold some of the work we needed to get done around the house if we wanted to sell. It was discouraging even though it became evident that God was just using it as a speed bump, not a road block. Now I can see it would have been bad timing to leave at that point. I needed to be assured I was leaving for the right reason. The right reason is following Jesus where He leads even when it makes little sense. The wrong reason would have been to get away from the hurt. Now that the bitterness was gone, I could see the value of the hurt. I could see how God had used it to heal me and grow me. The wounds were healing over, and the resulting scars had value.

The surgery was scheduled for about a month out. I made the mistake of telling my youngest. I thought I was pretty clear. "It's really not a big deal, but you don't need to go around telling people." I thought wrong.

She interpreted this to mean she should make it her Facebook status asking for prayer. She then added, "But I'm not allowed to tell you what the surgery is." Oh, and she tagged me in the post. It was awesome. I had a lot of curious people praying for me. Next time, I'll try to be more specific in my request for keeping her mouth shut, and her typing fingers quiet.

The surgery went without a hitch. One minute I'm being wheeled out of the pre-op room, the next minute I'm waking to a curious thing. There were two nurses moving aside the blanket around my feet to check out my ankles.

"What are you doing?" I asked. I thought this was the first thing I said since waking up. I was wrong. Way wrong.

"We just wanted to see the tattoo." the nurse answered.

So I let them check out my ankle, and asked, "How did you know I had a tattoo?"

Apparently I had been awake talking their ears off for quite a while. They heard all about the tattoo, and what it represents. It's a little Jesus fish with three crosses and the coloring of a sunset in the background. People are always trying to guess what it means. Apparently none of those people ever heard much about the crucifixion. I got it as a reminder to myself. There were two thieves with Jesus that day, one on either side of Him. One threw himself at the mercy of Jesus. The other mocked Him. In both cases Jesus let them, and respected their choices. It's a reminder to me each day, that I have a choice to make. And so does everybody else.

Now I guess it's a reminder to all the nurses in post-op because I'm told that I let them know they had a choice to make about Jesus just like my tattoo says. I don't remember any of what they told me, but it sure sounded like something I would say. It was nice to know that even under anesthesia, I was consistent. Conscious, unconscious, semi-conscious. Didn't seem to impede my testimony about Him. Apparently, I'm a Jesus freak through and through

When it was all said and done, the physical issue had been dealt with, and I was ready to move on. I think it's interesting to note that the spiritual healing, and with it the emotional healing, all occurred before the surgery. It preceded the physical remedy. Which tells me that it was mostly, or maybe totally, a spiritual problem. I have to give God props here. The thorn shaped polyp was a nice touch.

The rest of the summer was geared towards trying to have fun again. The previous summer had been a lost cause. This summer I was determined would be different. We had made plans to head to Disney and Universal in September. Until then we tried to make up for the lost summer. Ball games, amusement parks, trips to the lake and the beach. Life was feeling a lot calmer. I was feeling free again, and it was good.

We planned the Florida trip to attend Night Of Joy in Disney's Magic Kingdom. We had been for Night of Joy few years earlier. It was a great time of year to go to Disney. Most people pulling their kids out of school for a vacation wait until they're a few weeks into the year. As a result, most of the people you meet are either homeschoolers, or Florida residents coming over for the day. The crowds were light, the lines were short, the dining was free, and my favorite bands put on concerts in Magic Kingdom. This year we were adding a few days in Universal to the trip.

We had tickets to the first night of concerts. The line-up included Steven Curtis Chapman, Mercyme, and Rachel's favorite, Skillet. When Mercyme took the stage they sang, "Bring the Rain." This had been a song that God had used the previous summer to keep my heart in the right place. It was also lightly raining. The concert was one I was most excited about seeing. So of course my youngest had to go to the bathroom two songs into the concert.

We hurried through the crowds to get to the ladies room. We missed a few songs as we waited. I was feeling a little anxious about that. This was the band I most wanted to hear that night. We hurried out of the restroom, and ran up Main Street USA. When Cinderella's Castle was front and center, I heard the first few notes of The Hurt and The Healer. I stopped abruptly, and poor Olivia, who was holding my hand, was jerked back a little. I just had to stand there and worship God. Olivia was happy to hear they were good tears, and figured out we weren't hurrying back to everyone quite yet. As I stood there with tears in my eyes, I finally got it. Finally.

"It's the moment when humanity

Is overcome by Majesty

When Grace is ushered in for good

And all our scars are understood

When Mercy takes its rightful place

And all these questions fade away

When out of weakness we must bow

And hear You say "It's over now

I'm alive

Even though a part of me has died

You take my heart and breathe it back to life

I fall into Your arms open wide

When the hurt and the Healer collide"[6]

And there I was, standing in Magic Kingdom in front of Cinderella's castle finally really understanding some of those scars. That part of me that had died was clear now. And it needed to die. I was feeling free. It was a pretty cool moment. Did I mention I'm standing in front of Cinderella's Castle? I was.

The next day we decided the girls would go back for another night of Night of Joy, while the boys went out. I prayed that God would use us somehow that night. I was all set to dance down Main Street USA with Tobymac, much to Rachel's horror. He had been involved in so much kitchen dancing that Spring that it only seemed right to go. He put on a great show, and even Rachel had to admit that dancing a little was mandatory.

A few minutes before Tobymac came on stage, Rachel met a young woman. They bonded over a Hunger Games t-shirt. She said she worked at Hollywood Studios. She was meeting friends from work, but couldn't find them. Her story sounded a little fishy. She told us she was not a Christian, but loved Tobymac. I could see how that could happen if God was reeling someone in to Himself.

She was much more tolerant of my dancing tendencies than most people. She definitely knew the music. Still she was very open about the not being a Christian part. But she was one to let me talk. And she asked questions. Once again God was letting me be useful to someone He loved. I was able to share about God's healing, and that led to a familiar question. It's a question that makes me feel sad for those who ask it, but still strangely at peace.

Why? Why does God heal one person, and not another? He loves everybody, right? Why did God heal me, but not their loved one? Sometimes it's asked in anger, but mostly it's asked in honest confusion and grief. The problem is I'm not God so I don't know. I can see how He used the trial in our lives, but I can't explain why He took it out of me, and not others. I don't know, and I wonder about that myself.

She had the same question. Why would God heal me, but not her grandmother who was very sick? I had to tell her the truth: I didn't know. All I could do was testify about what He'd done for me.

She ended up hanging out with us after Tobymac finished. We went on a few rides together before the girls and I decided to head back to the hotel. As we parted ways, I asked her if I could pray for her. She said, "Yes," so I did. We were standing in Adventureland while I prayed for Angelica. I had one hand on her back, and one hand stretched to heaven as I prayed aloud for her heart to be opened to His salvation. When we left her she said, "Maybe I'll see you in heaven, after all." I hope so. She gave us her full name to look her up on Facebook. When I got home I tried to find her there, but I couldn't find her profile. Angelica had vanished just as randomly as she appeared. Hebrews 13:2 came to mind. Her name was Angelica after all.

It's amazing to me that in one short year, I can go from praising Jesus in the shower, to clinging to hope through a hopeless situation, to healing, and then on to foot stomping. When I stopped my whining and threw it back in His court, I found myself dancing down Main Street USA. Healthy, and whole and no longer angry. That right there is the real miracle.

Chapter 14: Lessons

What did I learn from all this? Well, I definitely gained perspective. I gained a deeper understanding of what it meant to follow Him. And also saw how easy it was to get sidetracked.

I was also set free. I didn't have to be wonder woman swooping in to always serve, and save the day. Life actually carried on just fine without me when I was out of commission. That was for everyone but my immediate family. My sights here on Earth needed to be more finely focused on them. I already knew this of course, but like many other things, He had to really show me, and smack me upside the head with it a few times in order for me to get it. Just like in the shower.

I had been spreading myself too thin, and He needed to straighten me out in dramatic fashion. I'm just that stubborn. Now I bet you may be thinking: She thinks she saw Jesus in the shower, and she heard voices. Maybe the alien abduction theory isn't so far off.

Don't worry, though. I don't think I saw Jesus in the shower, I know that I saw Him. Clearly none of the Renaissance artists ever saw Him. They were off on what He looks like. Even so, it was unmistakable who I saw. I knew it was Him, even though He didn't look like most imagine Him to look. And I don't hear voices. Just the one voice. The voice of God. Once you've met Him, it's unmistakable.

I found out I really do believe what I think I believe. When I was told I might be seeing God sooner rather than later, it was time to look mortality in the face. Did I really believe what I claimed to believe? It turned out that I did believe what I thought I believed. In fact I had no doubts. Death had no hold over me. This was good to know. That knowing will sustain me through whatever comes my way. I know where the end of the road will lead me. That certainty and eternal perspective will cover a multitude of trials.

It also confirmed in my heart the value and power of praising God. All the time. It doesn't matter what is happening in my life, I can still praise Him. He doesn't deserve my praise in the midst of a storm with the mindset of praising him "even though." I'll praise him just because of who He is. It doesn't really matter what is happening in my life. It's the only way to get through life in this broken world. He's still on the throne, and I can trust Him. Running to Him has never failed me.

If you don't know Him personally, you still may have heard Him. You may have mistaken Him for your conscience, though. We all like to take credit for what God's been doing. He's clear about His mission in speaking to unbelievers. He speaks to convict you of your sin against Him. Once you agree with Him, and throw yourself at His mercy, things will get very interesting. He'll have a lot more to say to you, and He'll blow your mind and rock your world on a frequent basis. It's so worth taking that leap of faith. Take a real look at yourself and throw yourself at the feet of Christ. He hung so you had that option. Take Him up on it. You'll never regret it.

If you're a believer reading this, and you've never heard the voice of God, you should be concerned. Very concerned. He speaks to His sheep. We don't always recognize it for what it is, or obey what He calls us to do, but He still speaks. He tells us in John 10 that His sheep know His voice. So it comes down to this: You either hear God speak to you in relationship, or you're not one of His sheep. He didn't really leave any room for debate about that.

He had me reading John 10 over and over again when I was sick that summer. He couldn't have been clearer with me in His faithfulness and longing for a real relationship. I was all for it when I was wandering in the valley, but after He lifted me up, I somehow let myself look the other way. Knowing now that I can go through what I went through with Him, and then so easily think I'm OK, and can start handling life on my own scares the daylights out of me. Reality is, I can't handle it on my own. I need Him.

You may have noticed that I don't hold much back when talking to God. In my experience, He's really OK with me being bold with Him, and telling Him what's on my mind. He already knows anyway! Just keep in mind He's still Lord of the universe. Treat Him as such, even as you revel in His presence. He's your friend, not your buddy. Keep perspective as you let Him have it all, because you're just you, and He's Him. It doesn't hurt to drop to your knees every now and then. Perspective is important.

As I'm sure you're aware, the death rate for humans is still holding steady at 100%. We'll all stand before Him one day. That's why deciding what to do with Jesus, is the most important decision you'll ever make. You can either stand before Him as the prodigal son welcomed home, or as a stranger who ran from Him every time He revealed Himself. He loves you enough to let you decide, but know that He will respect that decision. He won't force you to spend eternity with Him. You are free to choose an eternity separated from Him, but I wouldn't encourage it.

The eternity starts the moment you throw yourself at His mercy. You don't have to wait until you're dead to begin the journey. And let me tell you, God is fun, and funny. It'll be the ride of your life. Some of it we won't see until we die, but I did get a glimpse, and I can't wait to see it again.

For now the eternal life offers a major quality of life upgrade. I've lived it both ways: with Christ, and without Him. They don't even compare. With Him you can find hope in the midst of sorrow. Without Him there's just the sorrow. With Him there's peace in the chaos. Without Him there's just the chaos. With Him there's joy in the suffering. Without Him there's just the suffering. You see where I'm going here. There's no comparison. With Him you have abundant life. Without Him you'll just muddle through. Why muddle through when you can be lifted up?

Following isn't as easy as it could be. Even as someone who was already a follower, I looked away. When I was sick and looking at Him for everything, there was peace and joy in the middle of chaos. Then I got better and looked away. All I got from that was pain and a touch of misery. That is until He reeled me back in by His mercy.

It was kind of like Peter. When he got out of the boat with his eyes on Christ, he walked on water. Then he looked away. He looked at the wind and storm instead. That's when he started going down. Jesus pulled him up, but first He let him see what can happen when you look away. That's what happened to me. I was walking on water in a spiritual sense, despite my physical condition. And then I foolishly looked away. I don't recommend it.

If you're already a Christ follower, all I can say is this: Don't look away. Keep your eyes on Him. If you're not one already, you should really pursue Him. He'll make himself known if you truly call out to Him.

Epilogue

"Why are you telling me this?" I bet anyone reading this could be wondering that. I once shared just a brief snippet of this story with someone, and that was the reply. I found it to be a strange and depressing response. God had laid it on my heart to share with this woman, and that was what she had to say. Well, not all of it. She went on to tell me she didn't like me, and for some bizarre reason thought she already knew what I had shared. Considering no one but God and I were aware of the particulars of what I had shared, I'm not sure how she knew it. But clearly she was disappointed with the outcome. Once again I felt like someone wanted me to apologize for being healed. Didn't make me want to share my story again.

So why did God lay it on my heart to share with her? He knew what her reaction would be. He's God. Of course He knew. So why make me tell her? He must have been up to something. Needless to say, I have no idea what. Thankfully He doesn't hold me accountable for the unbelief of others, only my own.

Her response did make me wary of sharing, and I shut up about it for a while. So why am I telling YOU this? Here, too, I have no idea. Other than to say, "God told me to tell you." Repeatedly. That's all I've got. So please don't email me telling me that you never really liked me. That would be mean.

I'm sure He has a purpose. So be open to whatever that purpose might be. I do know that He's not surprised that you're reading this, and maybe, in fact probably, you're one of the reasons He made me write it down.

Endnotes

1. Louie Giglio, Chris Tomlin, John Newton, *Amazing Grace (My Chain Are Gone)* (Brentwood, TN: Sparrow Records, 2006), http.//www.azlyrics.com

2. Mark Hall, Bernie Hermes, *Praise You in This Storm,* (Nashville: Beach Street/Reunion, 2006), http.//www.azlyrics.com

3. Mark Hall, Steven Curtis Chapman, *Voice of Truth,* (Nashville: Beach Street, 2004), http.//www.azlyrics.com

4. Mike Donehey, Phillip LaRue, Jason Ingram, *Hold My Heart,* (Nashville: Centricity, 2008), http.//www.azlyrics.com

5. Jeremy Camp, *I Still Believe,* (Nashville: BEC Recordings, 2003), http.//metrolyrics.com

6. Bart Millard, Robby Shaffer, Jim Bryson, Mike Schuechzer, Nathan Cochran, Barry Graul, *The Hurt and The Healer,* (Brentwood, TN: Fair Trade, 2012), http.//www.azlyrics.com

7. Ed Cash, Scott Cash, Chris Tomlin, *Whom Shall I Fear[God of Angel Armies], (Brentwood, TN: Sparrow Records, , 2012),* http.//www.azlyrics.com

8. Jason Gray, Jason Ingram, *Remind Me Who I Am,* (Nashville: Centricity Music, 2011), http.//www.azlyrics.com

9. Mike Donehey, Jason Ingram, Jeff Owen, *Worn,* (Brentwood, TN: Reunion Records, 2012),), http.//www.azlyrics.com

10. Mike Donehey, *Losing,* (Brentwood, TN: Reunion Records, 2012), http.//www.azlyrics.com

11. Mike Donehey, Jason Ingram, Phillip LaRue, *By Your Side,* (Brentwood, TN, Reunion Records, 2008), http.//www.azlyrics.com

12. Bebo Norman, Jason Ingram, Mike Donehey, Jeffrey Stephen Norman, *Let it Go,* (Brentwood, TN, Reunion Records, 2008), http.//www.azlyrics.com

Made in the USA
Las Vegas, NV
07 September 2021